GW00537997

RACE ACROSS THE ATLANTIC

RACE ACROSS THE ATLANTIC

ALCOCK AND BROWN'S
RECORD-BREAKING NON-STOP FLIGHT

BRUCE VIGAR AND COLIN HIGGS

AIR WORLD

AIR WORLD

RACE ACROSS THE ATLANTIC
Alcock and Brown's Record-Breaking Non-Stop Flight

First published in Great Britain in 2019 by
Pen & Sword Air World
An imprint of
Pen & Sword Books Ltd
Yorkshire – Philadelphia

Copyright © Bruce Vigar and Colin Higgs, 2019

ISBN 978 1 52674 783 9

Typeset by Aura Technology and Software Services, India

Printed and bound in England by TJ International Ltd, Padstow, Cornwall

Pen & Sword Books Limited incorporates the imprints of Atlas, Archaeology, Aviation, Discovery, Family History, Fiction, History, Maritime, Military, Military Classics, Politics, Select, Transport, True Crime, Air World, Frontline Publishing, Leo Cooper, Remember When, Seaforth Publishing, The Praetorian Press, Wharncliffe Local History, Wharncliffe Transport, Wharncliffe True Crime and White Owl.

For a complete list of Pen & Sword titles please contact

PEN & SWORD BOOKS LIMITED
47 Church Street, Barnsley, South Yorkshire, S70 2AS, England
E-mail: enquiries@pen-and-sword.co.uk
Website: www.pen-and-sword.co.uk

Or
PEN AND SWORD BOOKS
1950 Lawrence Rd, Havertown, PA 19083, USA
E-mail: Uspen-and-sword@casematepublishers.com
Website: www.penandswordbooks.com

Contents

LONDON 2018

The first of October 2018 was not a good day for aviation as yet another airline went bust.

'European discount airline shuts down', 'Passengers left stranded', 'Collapse of budget airline sends rivals into a tailspin', screamed the headlines as another airline folded. It seems the airline in question, Primera Air, had overstretched its finances to provide low-cost travel across the Atlantic. Yet again, it was turmoil and chaos in the world of aviation that were making the headlines.

These days it is delays, drones, crowded terminals, lost luggage, noise, pollution and, very occasionally, disaster that grab the headlines. Interviews with angry, tearful, exhausted passengers are uploaded to social media and flashed round the world in seconds.

Aviation is itself a miracle. Every day thousands of passengers board aircraft in one continent and disembark on another having been flown in safety and comfort and without incident. Once in the air, we are carried in air-conditioned comfort at altitudes around 35,000 feet and at speeds approaching 550 miles per hour. We take the fact that we can traverse the globe in hours for granted, but it is often a demoralising, sometimes humiliating, and, just occasionally, a truly hellish experience.

Fifty years earlier, on 2 March 1969, Concorde made its first flight from Toulouse. Concorde was meant to herald in a new era of supersonic flight in which passengers would be transported across the Atlantic at twice the speed of sound, shortening the journey time by half. Concorde was a technical 'tour de force', the crowning achievement of the 'Jet Age' that could bring people together in record time. Breakfast in London, lunch in New York. Concorde flew higher than the other transatlantic flights. In fact, it flew so high that you could see the curvature of the Earth. How close to the future that must have felt. Aviation seemed to be on the threshold of a new and exciting era.

Three months later, on 20 July, the Apollo 11 mission put a man on the moon. The world held its breath as it watched live pictures of Neil Armstrong making those first tentative steps on the lunar surface. 'One small step for (a) man, one giant leap for mankind.' It seemed that there were few boundaries that human ingenuity, inventiveness and curiosity could not overcome.

Those words could have been the headlines fifty years earlier when on 15 June 1919 Captain John Alcock and Lieutenant Whitten Brown crash-landed their Vickers Vimy aircraft into a bog in western Ireland. Their achievement was as massive a step forward in aviation. In just ten years, aircraft that could barely cross the English Channel could now fly 1,900 miles across the Atlantic Ocean. The world needed new horizons and inspiration, a 'fresh start' after the numbing devastation of the First World War and the deadly 'flu epidemic that followed. It was as if mankind had turned a corner and that aviation would bring people together, inhabitants of a 'global village' in which disputes and misunderstandings could be overcome by talking face to face.

The idea that aviation could be a force for good was something that the aviators believed in (as well as the £10,000 prize put up by Lord Northcliffe, owner of the London *Daily Mail*). Sir Arthur Whitten Brown wrote about his ideas for transatlantic services at length. Indeed, Lord Northcliffe had been a passionate advocate of aviation, sponsoring a number of aviation events aimed at helping progress including Louis Blériot's crossing of the English Channel ten years before Alcock and Brown's Atlantic triumph.

Where Alcock and Brown led, others soon followed. A month after their flight, the R-34 Airship made the first east to west crossing in just over four days. After several days of celebrations, receptions and re-equipping, R-34 made the return crossing.

It was another eight years before the first solo crossing by Charles Lindbergh. Arguably his achievement has eclipsed that of Alcock and Brown in some quarters, but as he stepped out of his small aeroplane at Le Bourget in Paris, he acknowledged Alcock and Brown's achievement with the words:

'Alcock and Brown showed me the way.'

LONDON 1913

The Challenge

It could have been another April Fool prank. When at the beginning of April 1913 the London *Daily Mail* announced two aviation prizes totalling £15,000 pounds, there were the cynics from the dog-eat-dog world of newspapers who assumed the worst. It was not an unreasonable assumption, for the owner of the *Daily Mail* (and *Daily Mirror*) was Alfred Harmsworth, 1st Viscount Northcliffe, who did more than anyone to develop popular journalism intended for the (then) working classes. Sensationalist stories allied with aggressive marketing helped shape the popular journalism of today's tabloids.

But the *Daily Mail* had already provided several valuable prizes that encouraged aviation development.

Back in 1906, Viscount Northcliffe had joined the crowds in Paris to witness Brazilian aviator pioneer Albert Santos-Dumont fly his aircraft '14 bis' in a straight line for 220 metres. The *Fédération Internationale Aéronautique* immediately declared this to be a world record, choosing to ignore the Wright Brothers' claims to have flown further than this two years earlier. The spectacle left a deep impression on Viscount Northcliffe, leading him to declare with suitable tabloid hyperbole that 'England is no longer an Island.'

Over the next few years, the *Daily Mail* put up several prizes for competitions aimed at encouraging the fledgling world of aviation. It put up £1,000 for the first powered crossing of the English Channel, which was won by Frenchman Louis Blériot in 1909. There had been more: Circuit of Britain, Best Cross Country Aggregate and so on. All had played their part in pushing back the frontiers of flight as the prizes provided the kind of funding that early aviators needed to survive in the near-absence of official support.

The 1911 Circuit of Britain was a contest for the fastest completion of a course round Great Britain. The race was run from 22 July to 5 August and would cover a course of 1,010 miles with eleven compulsory stops on the way. The prize was £10,000 to the winner with several smaller prizes also on offer. In today's money, that is somewhere in the region of four million pounds, which is why the competitions were so eagerly followed. The competition rules and administration were run by the Royal Aero Club on behalf of the *Daily Mail*.

At a time when flying was still a rarity, twenty aviators entered in a variety of machines. Some like R.C. Fenwick crashed his Handley Page Type D even before the start. Just four finished the race and the winner was Lieutenant Jean Louis Conneau of the French Navy flying under the name of André Beaumont.

For the 1913 edition of the Circuit of Britain the rules were changed making it a race for floatplanes. The 1,540-mile course had to be completed in 72 hours. This time, the winner's prize was £5,000.

Aside from the technical challenges of building an aircraft capable of such a flight, there was the small matter of changing the Air Navigation Act which forbade flying over or near the British coast, except for about one twentieth of it and even that required special permission.

But the advances in aviation were such that it was likely that the prize would be won before the end of 1914.

In fact, there were no finishers and only one starter: Harry Hawker, who damaged his Sopwith while making an emergency landing near Dublin. As he had completed two thirds of the race the organisers decided to award him £1,000 for is efforts.

It was the second race, that was announced at the same time as the Circuit of Britain, that captured the headlines:

> **£10,000 to the** aviator who first crosses the Atlantic from any point in the United States of America, Canada, or Newfoundland to any point in Great Britain or Ireland in seventy-two continuous hours. The flight may be made, of course, either way across the Atlantic. This prize is open to pilots of any nationality, and machines of foreign or British construction.

The entry fee was £100 and the start could be made from land or water so long as the aircraft was airborne as it crossed the coast line. Similarly, landing could be on land or water. The challenge attracted attention from around the world with a number of aviation's pioneers registering their interest: Louis Blériot, American Colonel S.F. Cody who was pioneering flight with the British military, and Rumpler, the German manufacturer.

The challenge of crossing the Atlantic had already drawn a number of attempts, mostly in dirigible balloons. On 6 July 1912 it was reported that a second attempt to cross the Atlantic by dirigible had failed at the cost of five lives, including that of pilot Melvin Vaniman, who had been the main instigator of the latest attempt. The *Akron*, as the dirigible was called, was built by the Goodyear Rubber Co at Akron, Ohio, to Vaniman's design. It was only the airship's second flight when it was taken from its shed and steered out to sea. From an initial height of about 100 ft, the airship rose very rapidly to 1,000ft, apparently owing to the expansion of the gas caused by the heat of the sun. Suddenly the envelope was seen to explode, then flames burst out, and from the cloud of fire and smoke the car of the airship dropped into the sea. All the occupants must have been killed instantly.

Another German inventor, Beckmann, reckoned he could make the crossing in a hydro-aeroplane powered by two engines of his own design. He planned on flying from Spain's west coast to America with a fuel-stop in the Azores in thirty-seven hours.

But there were already two other attempts underway. Joseph Brucker was a German-American aviator who planned to fly from the Canaries to the West Indies in an enormous dirigible balloon called *Suchard II*. He planned

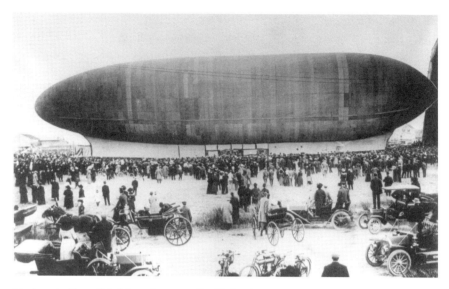

Vaniman's *Akron* dirigible at the start of its ill-fated attempt. (Library of Congress)

Suchard II was another balloon that failed to make the crossing.

to take three weeks of provisions as well as two assistants. However, despite papers reporting his imminent departure on 16 April, Brucker called off the attempt at the last minute.

On the other side of the Atlantic there had been much talk of an attempt being made by the American aviator and showman Harry N. Atwood.

American pioneer Harry N Atwood showed early interest in the race when it was first announced in 1913. (Library of Congress)

Atwood had been a student of the Wright Brothers and had stunned New Yorkers when he became the first aviator to fly over Manhattan's skyscrapers. He then thrilled the entire country when on 14 July 1911 he landed on the lawns of the White House and met US President William Taft.

By 1913 he was developing a plan to become the first aviator to cross the Atlantic. His hydro-aeroplane of his own design was to be powered by a single Renault engine producing around 70 horsepower. However, he was also going to have to carry around 250 gallons of fuel. His planned route was to fly from Boston to Saint John, New Brunswick, and from there to follow the shipping lanes to help him cover the 1,800 miles to the west coast of Ireland. He designed a pneumatic lifeboat with five watertight compartments which was to be attached to the lower wing by his cockpit.

Atwood had given the prospect of flying across the Atlantic a great deal of thought, and it has some resonance with Alcock and Brown's own experience six years later. He said, in an article in which he focussed less on the technical and logistical challenges but more on the physical hardship of the aviator, that the aviator would undoubtedly experience great difficulties in retaining his normal physical and mental equilibrium throughout many hours of relentless, nerve-racking vigilance – without for an instant escaping the deafening roar of the mighty engine. And for at least twenty-four hours he must sit in one position listening to the roar of that powerful engine, straining eyes through the daylight and darkness to keep in touch with all indications of trouble, enduring prolonged exposure to the elements and fighting off ever-increasing drowsiness. 'The length of the vigilance, together with the incessant and hypnotic roar of the engine, must sooner or later produce a physical and mental fatigue that will be well-nigh over-powering unless he has some means of fortifying himself against it.'

Even with fair winds to help him along, 250 gallons was not going to be enough to enable him to make the crossing. He went to see President Taft to present his case that the US Navy might like to help bridge the gap by positioning vessels along the route so that he could put down on the sea and be refuelled from a ship.

Taft refused him saying that the US Navy was not going to be used as an ocean-going filling station. Furthermore, if disaster struck, the navy would stand accused of aiding the death of a civilian, and if Atwood succeeded, the glory would be his alone.

Atwood was not alone in recognising the problem of fuel supply. There was simply no aero-engine in existence that could provide the range and power necessary to cross the Atlantic.

Others noted the navigational challenges in such a journey. A compass alone was not accurate enough – a pilot could be as much as fifty miles off course and be none the wiser unless there was some means of getting a fix on something below; not easy in the great expanse of the ocean. The centuries-old technique of astro-navigation would certainly help, but this relied on clear skies to get a fix.

Rodman Wanamaker was a pioneer in sponsoring record-breaking aviation projects, transatlantic flight development in particular. In 1913 he commissioned Glen Curtiss and his aircraft company to further develop his experimental flying boat designs into a scaled-up version capable of transatlantic crossing. The result was the Curtiss Model H, christened *America*, which first flew on 22 June 1914. The flying boat was developed under British designer John Cyril Porte's supervision who also acted a chief test pilot. After initial problems the *America* was ready to make the flight across the Atlantic. August 5th was the date chosen, to take advantage of a full moon. But the flight never took place because of the outbreak of the First World War.

Any notion that aviation could bring people together by overcoming geographic distance was dashed when the First World War began, and the competition suspended. It seemed that the *Daily Mail*'s £10,000 was safe for the foreseeable future.

The war was to have a profound impact on aviation. At the start, aircraft were limited by range and performance to spotting for the artillery and reconnaissance. It was not long before they became fighting machines as each side sought to deny the other the ability to see the disposition of their forces. Winning the battle for the skies became an objective in its own right. Aircraft that were specifically designed for air combat were built. Small, agile and fast, their job was to get airborne quickly and shoot down as many enemy aircraft as possible. As the opposing sides were rarely more than a few miles apart, there was little requirement for endurance. This was just as well as aero-engines were very unreliable and difficult to operate. For example, many aircraft adopted the radial rotary engine layout in which the entire engine block and propeller rotated round a fixed crankshaft. At this early stage, the large frontal area was quite effective at keeping the engine cool. It also had a better power-to-weight ratio than 'conventional' engines as there was no need for additional items like fly-wheels to smooth out the engine's vibrations. But all that weight spinning in one direction meant that the aircraft was usually very good at turning in one direction but reluctant to turn in the other. On engines like the widely used Gnome, there was barely any throttle control; the engine was either 'on' or 'off'. Engine power could be reduced for landing by using an ignition interrupter device which cut the spark to alternate spark plugs. Of course, the non-firing cylinders would still draw fuel and so fires were not uncommon. Thus landing these machines required training as well as great skill, which, given the short life-expectancy of pilots on the Western Front, they rarely got. Aircraft like the Sopwith Camel were notorious for sending inexperienced pilots spinning into the ground, such was the violence of the gyroscopic effect and the tendency for the nose to dip when power was applied. On the other hand, this gyroscopic effect was effective in air combat as the pilot could simply flick the Camel all the way round, making it one of the most manoeuvrable combat aircraft of the war.

But the days of the rotary engine were numbered as they simply could not produce enough power. Making them bigger induced too much drag. Also, they used a lot of oil and it was not possible to get enough oil fed to the larger cylinders. New metals meant that in-line, water-cooled engines were improving, but were still mainly used on larger aircraft.

The air war was evolving in other areas. Aerial attacks on London and other British cities brought civilians into the front line for the first time in centuries. At first the Germans used Zeppelins which in favourable weather could turn their engines off, silently drift towards their target and mount a surprise attack.

In May 1917 the Germans mounted the first air raids using Gotha bombers. These were powered by twin Mercedes engines. However, reliability was poor, and many had to turn back with mechanical problems.

Britain had also experimented with larger multi-engine aircraft led, arguably, by Handley Page. The O/100 which first flew in December 1915 was the first of a series of increasingly powerful aircraft culminating in the O/1500. The O/100 and its successor the O/400 were mainly used for attacking targets from bases in France or anti-shipping and U-Boat operations in the North Sea. But the O/1500 was designed to strike Berlin from a base in England. Much of this new-found capability was due to the Rolls Royce Eagle Mark VIII aero engine.

The Rolls-Royce Eagle was the company's first aero engine. It began life following a request that the company develop an air-cooled engine that could deliver 200 horsepower. Initially, the company was reluctant but agreed to develop an engine so long as it could be water-cooled as this was their area of expertise.

Henry Royce led the development of the 20-litre engine from his home in Kent. His first design drew on the 7.4 litre 40/50 Rolls Royce 'Silver Ghost' auto engine as well as the 7.2 litre Daimler DF80 aero engine which had been used in the Mercedes Grand Prix cars for 1913. Royce was able to increase power output by doubling the number of cylinders to twelve and giving them a longer stroke while retaining the same bore as the Silver Ghost engine. Performance was also improved by adopting a single overhead cam design for the valve train.

Although the engine had not yet been run, the Admiralty placed an initial order for twenty-five engines in January 1914. The following month, the Eagle was run for the first time at the Rolls-Royce works in Derby. Straight away the engine exceeded specifications, producing 225hp at 1,600rpm. By mid-1915 this had been increased to 2,000rpm and produced 300hp. However, for production it was decided to restrict the engine to 1,800 rpm and 225hp. Throughout the war, the Eagle was continuously developed and by 1918 the Mark VIII version was producing 360hp.

The Eagle was a very successful aero engine and was much in demand by the War Office. But Rolls-Royce refused to licence other manufacturers to build their engines as they feared the Eagle's much-admired quality would be compromised.

After the war, Rolls-Royce continued to build Eagles for the civilian market until 1928. The Eagle was to play a prominent role in the race to be the first to fly non-stop across the Atlantic.

DOVER

16 December 1918

As the ship slid into Dover's ancient harbour, men crowded the decks. Even the rain could not dampen their spirits as they gazed on the towering white cliffs and the castle above the port. To a man they had longed for this moment, dreamt of it as they lay on their mean bunks waiting as all prisoners must do for time to pass. It was a spirit-sapping experience. As prisoners of war, they had no idea how long they would have to wait – weeks? Months? Years? Perhaps they might not see home again. But such thoughts were now gone amongst the men as they waited impatiently for dock lines to be secured and gang planks positioned. The time of year gave the atmosphere an added piquancy. Not only were they heading home, they were heading home for Christmas. For the first time in years they would be home in time to spend this most special time of the year with their families, to tell their tales and swop stories with new friends and acquaintances over a pint, reliving over and over what had happened in answer to the same question 'What was it like'?

There would be sadness too. The news of friends and relatives who would not be coming back, whose Christmases would forever be a quiet affair in the corner of a foreign field while their families struggled to reconcile their loss with the joy of this first Christmas without war.

The world the men were coming home to was very different to the one they had left behind. There had been a general election just days before their return, the first election in which women could both vote and stand as candidates. More women were going out to work than ever before and many were not going to give up their hard-won independence just because their menfolk were returning from war.

Once ashore there were the dreary formalities to go through for the umpteenth time: name, rank, date of birth and so on before they could begin the final stage of their homecoming.

Amongst the cheery throng stood Captain John William Alcock DSC, known as Jack to his family and friends. Even before the war Alcock had built his reputation as one of the country's best pilots having gained the coveted Royal Aero Club licence by the time he was 20.

His reputation had been burnished further by war, before mechanical failure brought him crashing down and fourteen months of captivity. It was while idling away the long hours of captivity that he hatched his grand plan to become the first aviator to fly the Atlantic.

Born on 5 November 1892 in Stretford, Greater Manchester, he went to schools in Stockport and Lytham St Annes. Growing up, he showed an interest in all things mechanical and this led to an early interest in aviation. His first job was as an apprentice at the Empress Motor Works in Manchester on the Stockport Road at Longsight. Empress built aeroplanes and rotary engines designed by the works manager Charles Fletcher who was a keen aviator and Norman Crossland, a motor engineer and founder of the Manchester Aero Club. It was during this time that Alcock met French aviator Maurice Ducrocq, who was a demonstration pilot and UK agent for aero engines made by the Italian Spirito Mario Viale.

Ducrocq took Alcock on as a mechanic at his factory at the Brooklands aerodrome in Surrey where he learnt to fly in Ducrocq's flying school. In November 1912 he was awarded his pilot's certificate by the Royal Aero Club. After that, Alcock started getting noticed on the air racing scene, often piloting a Maurice Farman biplane powered by an eight-cylinder, water-cooled Sunbeam engine.

But with the outbreak of war, all attempts at records and air racing competitions came to an abrupt end.

Alcock volunteered as an instructor in the Royal Naval Air Service and with the rank of captain was sent to Eastchurch on the Isle of Sheppey to train naval pilots. His Farman went with him as both men and machines were in short supply. In the beginning, little thought had been given to how aviation might fit into a military role. But with hard work they overcame the difficulties and shortage of machines and started to produce well-trained pilots. Among them was Sub-Lieutenant R.A.G. Warneford, who was awarded the Victoria Cross but was killed soon after shooting down the first Zeppelin.

Although it was a necessary role, Alcock found instructing frustrating work as he wanted to be in the thick of it, in action. He was delighted therefore when he received instructions to proceed to Romania for active duty. But he never reached that front, as he was sent instead to Mudros on the Greek island of Lemnos. There he got all the action he could have wished for. Much of the time they flew Sopwith Camels, and Alcock was credited with downing seven enemy aircraft for which he was awarded the Distinguished Service Cross.

He managed to find time to indulge his passion for things mechanical, building his own scout using parts salvaged from wrecked machines. By his own reckoning, Alcock thought it would be a potent little fighter, but he never got to find out as the machine was destroyed when an aircraft returning from a night-time flight landed on top of it in the darkness completely destroying it.

These were busy times, and although Alcock was ostensibly a fighter pilot he also flew bombing sorties, often flying for over eight hours to reach distant targets such as Constantinople, Adrianople, Panderma and the Dardanelles.

On 30 September 1917 Alcock's wartime career took a dramatic turn. The day had started well. While on patrol he encountered two German aircraft providing cover for a third, a reconnaissance machine. He shot the first escort down, but the second proved more elusive. However, his tenacity paid off and he sent the second aircraft down into the Aegean (from where the pilot was rescued). He must have been desperate because he scribbled a last message to his girlfriend in large letters on one of the propeller blades which was picked up later by a British crew. Surprisingly, following his Atlantic flight in 1919, Alcock received a letter from a Bulgarian lady, Straoka Ilievna, who was the former girlfriend of the pilot. She had seen Alcock's photo in the *Daily Mirror* in which he was posing with the propeller with the message to her.

Later that day, Alcock and two crew climbed aboard a Handley Page O/100 bomber for a raid on Constantinople. While over enemy lines on the Gallipoli peninsula, the reduction gear sheared off Alcock's aircraft, possibly due to anti-aircraft fire. One engine failed immediately. They managed to continue on one engine, covering sixty miles before that also failed. With no alternative, they were forced to ditch in the sea off Suvla Bay. As they clung to the wreckage, they were sniped at by Turks on the shore.

As the wreck was starting to sink and there was no prospect of being rescued, Alcock and his crew decided to seek the comparative safety of the land. They swam for an hour before washing up exhausted on the rocky shore. There they lay, hiding in what cover they could find. By noon the following day, exhaustion was taking its toll and they decided to surrender. They were soon picked up by a patrol who stripped them of everything of value including their clothes. They were then marched off to the Turks' camp at gunpoint. Physically drained and mentally stressed by their situation, they were very relieved to be well received by the camp's commander. Apart from a little money, all their clothes were returned, and they were given a meal which went a long way to restoring their spirits.

For the next stage of his incarceration, Alcock was transferred to Constantinople. There he met Mehmet Cavit Bey, the Finance Minister who promised him good treatment but, as a temporary measure, he would be held in a local jail. Whatever Alcock and crew were expecting, the jail was to prove a grim experience. Food was scarce, what they had was generally bad, and they feared starvation. Their cell was overrun by vermin, and it was possibly during this time that he picked up a malaria-like infection that would return after the war. Also, they were tormented daily by being told that they would be moved the following day. To their jailers, 'tomorrow' was always on the horizon. This went on for a month before they were able to get a message to Mehmet Cavit Bey who responded immediately by having them moved to Kedos, a prisoner of war camp in western Anatolia. Unlike the Germans and Austro-Hungarians, the Turks did not build concentration camps for their prisoners, preferring to billet them in houses in the town, often those previously occupied by Armenians. At Kedos, although sanitary conditions were poor, they had access to a theatre, they could run classes, and they had a sports field for football and hockey. What was more, they could receive Red Cross parcels containing little luxuries such as chocolate and soap. Officers were allowed to walk up to five kilometres from the town if they gave their parole they would not try to escape.

With time on his hands, Alcock began thinking about the Atlantic challenge. He had confidence in his own ability to fly long distances at night but what machines would be capable of such a flight? But the routine of camp life was disrupted once more, first by an outbreak of influenza, and then in September 1918 a great fire that swept through the town destroying 2,000 of the 2,300 homes in Kedos. Although the British were given credit for their attempts at fighting the fire, and then spending a month out in the open, there was little alternative but to move them to a new camp. As the end of the war was in sight, they were transferred to a camp at Smyrna (present-day Izmir) ready for repatriation.

The journey home was long and arduous. Leaving Turkey on 18 November, Alcock travelled first from Smyrna to Alexandria and then to Cairo. From Cairo he sailed for England, arriving back on home soil on 16 December. As he headed home to his parents and brothers and sister he reflected what a wonderful time this was to be back at home for Christmas, coming so soon after the Armistice celebrations. This would be a Christmas the Alcock family would never forget.

Meanwhile, another Manchester family were making preparations for the coming holiday. But for Arthur Whitten Brown, the future looked

Capt John Alcock. (BAE Systems)

less rosy. He wanted to marry Marguerite Kathleen Kennedy, one of his boss's daughters, but he now faced unemployment as his job in the Ministry of Munitions was redundant now that the war was over. What was more, the cold damp weather made his leg hurt, the result of a war wound. Nevertheless, he resolved to double his efforts to find a job in the new year.

Arthur Whitten Brown was born on 23 July 1886 in Glasgow to American parents, Arthur George Brown and his wife Emma Whitten. Arthur was an electrical engineer who had moved to Scotland to find a site for a new Westinghouse factory. While the young Arthur, also known as 'Teddy', was still an infant the family moved to Manchester after it was decided to open the new Westinghouse factory at Trafford Park. This was very near John Alcock's birthplace, although their paths appear not to have crossed while growing up in Manchester.

The young Arthur evidently inherited his father's enthusiasm for engineering as he became an apprentice at British Westinghouse which, by his own account, he thoroughly enjoyed. He then found himself working in South Africa until the outbreak of war.

All that changed with the outbreak of war in 1914 when he returned to England to enlist. As he was an American citizen, Brown had to take out British citizenship. He joined the University and Public Schools Brigade whose ranks were full of potential officers. Brown was one of those who sought a commission and became a second lieutenant in the 3rd (Special Reserve) Battalion of the Manchester Regiment. After seeing service in the trenches at Ypres and the Somme, he volunteered to join the Royal Flying Corps as an observer. It was while spotting for the artillery over the Somme battlefield that Brown's aircraft from No 2 Squadron RFC was shot down by anti-aircraft fire over Vendin le Vielle. The aircraft was set partially alight, but he and the pilot managed to make a crash landing. They were battered and bruised as well as suffering burns and as a result were sent back to England to recuperate.

When Brown returned to France he resumed his duties as an observer on 2 Squadron RFC. On 10 November he took off in a B.E.2c reconnaissance machine with pilot Lieutenant Henry Medlicott for what turned out to be their last sortie. Again they were shot down, but this time a bullet had pierced the fuel tank forcing them to crash land behind German lines. Brown sustained a serious leg injury which was to plague him for the rest of his life. Both men were taken prisoner. Medlicott went on to achieve notoriety as the most prolific escaper of the war. But he never made it home. Following another failed attempt – his fourteenth – Medlicott was executed by his guards.

Brown was held prisoner at Clausthal in the Harz mountains. Like all prisoners, once the initial misery of being captured had passed, time began to drag for Brown as he lay on his bed at night, unable to sleep because of the pain in his leg. He began thinking about aerial navigation and the challenges that long-distance flight posed. He was allowed books on navigation supplied by the Red Cross which he read voraciously, and he began to think about Lord Northcliffe's prize and how he might lay claim to be the first to fly the Atlantic.

His leg was taking its time to heal, and on 18 January 1917 he was transported to

Lieutenant Arthur Whitten Brown. (BAE Systems)

The POW camp Kurhaus Pfauenteich hotel at Clausthal where Brown was held. (BAE Systems)

```
                                      Liste reçue le 23.1.17
          Transport du 18 janvier 1917 - Anglais.
          ---------------------------------------------
             Région Château d'Oex.                FS 1669
          -------------------------

Sydney, Jackson      Colonel    Hampshire Regt. Villingen
Earl of Stair John   Major      Scots Guards        "
Simpson Charles      Major      Gordon Highl.       "
Young Frederic       Major      Cheshire Rgt.       "
Löwe Percival        Capitaine  West-Yorkshire Regt. Klausthal Nervenschw.
Brown Arthur         Lieutenant Manchester Rgt.     "        Herzleiden
                                                             Fussverw.
Frost Arvey              "      Royal Sbyr Corps    "        Oberschkl.-
                                                             Verwundung
Hamil John           Soldat     Scott Wod.Rgt. Hammelburg  lk.O.Arm
Underhill Thomas       "          "    "    "      "        r. O.Schenkel
Harkmann Thapa         "        4.Gurkha      Wünsdorf      r.Auge verloren
Dalbahadur Thapa       "        2/8.Gurkha       "          L. "       "
Sakak Khan             "        69.Scind.Rifles   "         r. "       "
Mazullah Khan          "        69.Punjabis       "         r. "       "
Ahmed Khan             "        69.  "            "         l. Hand gelähmt
```

Arthur Whitten Brown was repatriated via Switzerland in 1917. The log records that he had a 'foot wound' which was to plague him for the rest of his life but also some sort of heart problem. (IRC Archives)

16

Château d'Oex in Switzerland as part of a repatriation programme brokered by the Red Cross. He finally arrived back in England on 11 September. Although he was fit enough to fly, Brown found employment in the Ministry for Munitions until the end of the war. It was while he worked there that he first met Kathleen Kennedy.

On 10 March 1919 John Alcock was demobilised from the Royal Air Force. His desire to fly burned as brightly as it ever had and he wasted little time before going back to his old stamping ground at Brooklands looking for work. A man of his reputation and experience was just what Vickers were looking for and he was taken on as a test pilot. His arrival could not have been more timely as Vickers were considering taking part in the most risky but potentially rewarding challenge that would define the age: to be the first to fly non-stop across the Atlantic.

THE TEAMS

The 1918 Armistice brought peace to a world that would never be the same again. Thousands of men – and women – had learned to drive or ride motorcycles as part of their war work. People other than the wealthy could travel further, whether for work or leisure. War had also seen huge advances in aircraft design, and more specifically in aero engine design. Aircraft were still mostly biplanes made of wood, wire and canvas, but the endurance, performance and reliability of aero engines meant that aircraft could now fly from England to Berlin and back.

But with peace came the 'Peace Dividend'. The valuable government orders that had financed the aircraft manufacturers which in turn funded the design and development of new aircraft more or less dried up overnight. The future for the manufacturers and their thousands of employees depended on finding new uses for aircraft. Small, fast, single-engine fighters were of little use outside their military roles, but the larger bombers could be modified to carry passengers so opening up the world of civil transport. Although the *Daily Mail*'s prize was of enormous value, the publicity and prestige of being the first to fly non-stop across the Atlantic was of far greater value.

Following the end of the war in 1918, the Royal Aero Club lifted its ban on Atlantic flying and the *Daily Mail* reinstated the competition. The British government did not show much interest in supporting a national effort and so it was left to Britain's aircraft manufacturers to make their own minds up about whether to enter or not. Many chose not to as the risks were seen as too great. Initially there were eleven entries, but most fell by the wayside and never even got as far as building an aircraft let alone transporting it across to Newfoundland, the most easterly part of the United States from where they would be able to take advantage of the prevailing winds that blew eastwards.

Just five British teams made the attempt: Vickers-Armstrong, Sopwith, Martinsyde, Handley-Page, and Short Brothers. Others that took a serious look at the possibilities were most notably Boulton & Paul, Fairey Aviation and the Alliance Aeroplane Co. But the competition also drew interest from abroad.

SUNDSTEDT

Captain Hugo Sundstedt was a Swedish aviator and pioneer who, one month before the outbreak of the First World War, met the Anglo-French pioneer Henri Farman in Paris and bought one of his biplanes. He flew the Farman back to Sweden, covering some 1,180 miles and flew non-stop for 13 hours and 20 minutes – a tremendous feat of endurance. During the war he was to undertake another eight flights of over 1,000 miles.

At the beginning of 1917 he arrived in New York City and had the good fortune to meet the incredibly wealthy Christoffer Hannevig Jr. He persuaded Hannevig to back his project and together they approached the Witteman-Lewis Aircraft Company of New Jersey to build an enormous float plane designed by Sundstedt.

Named the Sundstedt-Hannevig *Sunrise,* it was a huge aircraft for its time. Its upper wing spanned 100 feet. However, its empty weight was 7,000 lbs, less than half the 15,874 lbs of the comparably sized US Navy Curtiss NC-4 which was to make the Atlantic crossing in a series of hops via the Azores. Fully loaded with fuel and crew the contrast was even more remarkable: its 13,000 lbs was less than half the weight of the NC-4's 28,000 lbs.

The *Sunrise* had two six-cylinder Hall-Scott engines, each rated at 220 hp, mounted so that they faced rearwards to push the aircraft through the air. These engines were a lot smaller than the Liberty or Rolls-Royce engines which were powering aircraft of similar size. Indeed the NC-4 had four 400-hp Liberty V-12s and carried 1,891 gallons of fuel, weighing more than 11,000 lbs.

Smaller engines consumed less fuel. The *Sunrise* carried a single 750-gallon tank of gasoline (and 100 gallons of oil). Sundstedt calculated that this was sufficient for 20-22 hours of flight. At the aircraft's calculated cruising speed of 80 mph, this gave the aircraft a range of 1,600-1,760 miles.

This might sound marginal at best, because he would have to cover the 1,700 miles of Atlantic Ocean that lay between St John's, Newfoundland, and Queenstown in Ireland. But Sundstedt had also studied German military data concerning the North Atlantic which gave him an insight into the existence, strength and direction of air currents which we now recognise as the fringes of the jet stream.

He learnt that there were air currents of 50 to 75 mph that flowed west to east at an altitude of 10,000 feet. He also identified their path, which was further north than the lanes traditionally followed by the steamships that crisscrossed the Atlantic. Therefore he was confident (as were others attempting the west-to-east crossing) that he would pick up significant speed from the tailwinds expected along this northern passage. His calculations were to prove correct.

Sundstedt seemed to have everything in place to make the first non-stop Atlantic crossing. He had the funding which enabled him to start preparing early. He also had a viable aircraft and a well-thought-through flight plan. The one ingredient he lacked was luck.

On 1 March 1919, the *Sunrise* was ready to begin flight testing before flying up to St John's. From there Sundstedt planned to launch his Atlantic challenge.

Sitting on her mooring in Newark Bay, the engines were found to be incorrectly set at differing rpm. *Sunrise* started drifting before hitting a small landing dock, damaging a wing. A few days later they made a second attempt. This time the engines refused to fire up, leaving *Sunrise* to drift around Newark Bay once again with her crew chilled to the bone.

Sundstedt took things in his stride: 'These things always happen when a new plane is tried out. They are flea bites. I am in no hurry to get started, except that I must start before anyone else does.'

Eventually *Sunrise* did get airborne again, but again disaster struck. While banking to come into land, *Sunrise* went into a sideslip. At 300 ft there was no room to recover. This time the damage was more serious. In fact it was so serious that Sundstedt said that the accident had in effect eliminated his machine from the race. He said: 'It will require at least a month to construct new pontoons and by that time some of the present entries undoubtedly will have made the flight.' How right he was.

Above left: Hugo Sundstedt's 'Sunrise' under construction. (Library of Congress)

Above right: Hugo Sundstedt standing on one of the floats provides a sense of scale. (Library of Congress)

Below: The Sundstedt 'Sunrise' was an enormous aircraft designed to carry 4 people. (Library of Congress)

The 'Sunrise' under construction at the Witteman-Lewis Aircraft Co. in New Jersey. (Library of Congress)

SOPWITH AND HAWKER

Sopwith had built a formidable reputation as a builder of very successful fighters, or 'scouts' as they were called. Aircraft like the Sopwith Triplane and Camel had played an important part in swinging the air war in the Allies' favour. In 1914 the company employed 200 personnel, by 1918 this had risen to 6,000. Over 16,000 aircraft were built by the factory alone, more were built under licence by other manufacturers.

The Sopwith entry was to be led by test pilot Harry George Hawker.

By 1919, Hawker was already a household name thanks to a long list of aviation achievements. His rise had been rapid. Born in Melbourne, Australia, in 1889, Hawker showed a flair for mechanics at an early age. By 1911 he had saved up enough money to come to England where he hoped to learn to fly. At just 5ft tall he looked a lot younger than his 22 years and was easily dismissed as an over-ambitious child. By July he was about to give up and return home when he landed a job at the Commer Car Company. He soon

Harry Hawker MBE AFC was idolised by the public and royalty alike. He was tragically killed in a flying accident in 1921. (Library of Congress)

demonstrated his considerable skills as an engineer and mechanic. By 1912 he was working for Mercedes when a chance introduction to Fred Sigrist, Sopwith's chief foreman, provided the opportunity he needed. He was soon working for Sopwith as a mechanic at their Brooklands factory. Hawker was so eager to learn to fly that legend has it that he spent his first wages on flying lessons. He proved to be a natural aviator. After just three lessons, he flew solo for over fifty minutes. In September he gained his Royal Aero Club licence, No. 297, and to cap it all, Tom Sopwith appointed him as the company's test pilot after he had set a new endurance record of over eight hours. His flying achievements made him a household name and his adoring public followed his every exploit, including, it is said, the King. Even his aborted attempt to win the 1914 Circuit of Britain was guaranteed to garner plenty of column inches in the daily papers.

Although Hawker volunteered for military service he was turned down as his testing work was of greater importance.

Hawker liked to whistle while he worked and had long fingers that twitched noticeably. It was said that this was down to his various testing injuries. When things were not going well, he could be sharp and irritable as he tried to solve a mechanical problem. At night his wife Muriel read to him, first the aviation and auto publications and then teenage adventure stories.

Hawker was to be joined on the attempt by navigator Lieutenant Commander Kenneth Mackenzie-Grieve. Grieve, now 39, had followed family tradition and joined the Royal Navy at 14. During the war he served aboard the seaplane tender *Campania* as navigation officer. It was this experience that got him interested in flying. He was then loaned to the newly-formed Royal Air Force when the Sopwith Company asked if he could work with Hawker.

Grieve (navigator) and Hawker (pilot) In front of their Sopwith 'Atlantic'.

Their aircraft was a specially built Sopwith, named *Atlantic*. Designed by George Carter, it was based on the manufacturer's experimental B1 bomber, two of which had been built. It was specially modified for the Atlantic bid and supposedly could fly 3,000 miles on the amount of fuel it could carry, more than enough for the ocean jump. Powered by a single Rolls-Royce Eagle engine it had already flown more than 1,800 miles in test flights, as the aviators munched on sandwiches made by Hawker's wife Muriel. But at 6,150 pounds, fully loaded, Sopwith engineers weren't so confident. They modified the *Atlantic* so that the undercarriage could be dropped once Hawker was airborne. Of course that created another problem: how were they to land in Ireland? That conundrum was never answered, the objective was to just get there, and they would worry about landing later.

With the weight reduced, and the increase in speed of seven miles per hour coupled with a favourable tail wind, they thought they could reach Fermoy in Ireland, a journey of 2,000 miles.

On this transatlantic adventure, Hawker planned to crash in Ireland, hopefully safely and in one piece. A belly landing on land was considered a lesser threat than setting down in the ocean, but the engineers had taken

The Sopwith's offset navigator's cockpit and the detachable rear section of fuselage are clearly visible. (BAE Systems)

that possibility into account too: they designed the aft part of the fuselage into a small, detachable, two-man boat (although how long it could have remained afloat in the Atlantic swell is open to question). They also provided rubberised suits that MacKenzie-Grieve and Hawker could pull on while awaiting rescue

MARTINSYDE

The next team to make the journey to Newfoundland was the Martinsyde team headed by Frederick Phillips Raynham and Major C.W.F. Morgan.

Raynham was a familiar name to the British public and was one of the early British aviators to gain a Royal Aero Club permit (9 May 1911). He was one of the first pilots to survive a spin and successfully land his aircraft in one piece. By 1912, Raynham was instructor and manager at the Sopwith school at Brooklands although he did not stay there long. He had set his sights on winning the British Empire Michelin Trophy No 1, awarded to the British pilot who could remain airborne the longest in a single flight in an all-British aircraft. The flight had to be completed between sunrise and one hour after sunset. On 24 October 1912 Raynham took off in an enclosed

Frederick Phillip Raynham OBE (1893 – 1954) One of the great early aviation pioneers also known as 'unlucky' as he always seemed to miss out on the big prizes often to Hawker or Alcock. His generosity to Alcock and Brown in allowing them to use his airfield and fuel enabled them to make their flight before Handley Page and Raynham himself. (Library of Congress)

Avro biplane at dawn. His rival for this prestigious prize was Harry Hawker who took off a little later in a Sopwith-Wright biplane. After 7½ hours flying, Raynham's machine ran out of oil. It seemed to matter little as he had smashed the existing record by some margin. But Hawker was still airborne and kept flying until he landed after sunset, having flown for 8 hours and 23 minutes. This was not to be the only time that Raynham was to see defeat snatched from the jaws of victory, and not the only time by Harry Hawker. He was also a friend of John 'Jack' Alcock as their paths often crossed either when competing in air races or testing new aircraft.

During the First World War Raynham continued as a test pilot. It was a role for which he seemed to have an insatiable appetite despite accidents along the way.

For the Atlantic challenge he was to be joined by Major C.W.F. Morgan as navigator. Their aircraft was a Martinsyde F4 Buzzard re-named *Raymor*, a combination of their two names. The *Raymor* began life in 1917 as a design for a new fighter – or 'scout' as they were then referred to. Designed

Raynham and Morgan's Martinsyde 'Raymor' was heavily loaded and was unable to take off. (NARA)

by George Handasyde of Martinsyde, the new aircraft, designated the 'F3', was powered by a single Rolls-Royce Falcon engine. During initial trials, with a maximum speed of 142 mph, it proved much faster than other scouts in service. But Rolls-Royce could not supply enough Falcons as they were needed for another new aircraft, the Bristol Fighter. The solution was to fit the Hispano-Suiza '8' engine. Redesignated the F4 Buzzard, large orders were placed by the Royal Air Force and French Air Force, and as well as 1,500 for the United States. But just as production was getting under way, the Armistice was declared and the orders were cancelled. Martinsyde started buying back the surplus aircraft and converting them to two-seat aircraft for long range flights, powered once more by the Rolls-Royce Falcon. One of these was the *Raymor* for Raynham and Morgan's Atlantic attempt.

WHITEHEAD AIRCRAFT

When, at the end of the war, the *Daily Mail* Trans-Atlantic Flight £10,000 prize was announced, Whitehead Aircraft Limited was the first to submit an entry. Captain A. Payze was named as the pilot and the yet-to-be-designed machine was to have a wing span of 120 feet and be powered by four Liberty engines each producing 400hp. On paper, this not only looked technically viable but also superior to the other contenders.

RACE ACROSS THE ATLANTIC

The company had been founded by John Alexander Whitehead who had made and then lost a fortune in timber in the United States. Determined to find another fortune he returned to England in 1914. As his stated occupation was 'carpenter', and he was certainly a good judge of timber, he was employed by the Aircraft Manufacturing Company building Farmans under licence for flying schools. It was while there that Whitehead thought he ought to be building aircraft in his own factory. He managed to secure premises in Richmond, Surrey, and then approached the War Office as it was in need of new contractors as the Admiralty had already monopolised the established aircraft factories for its own needs. An order for six B.E.2bs was issued to test the firm's capabilities. The first aircraft passed its inspections but a new order for 100 Maurice Farman Shorthorns quickly followed. The fact that his workshop, in what had been a former drill hall, had received such a substantial order can only be attributed to his skill in selling himself. A new factory was built at Hanworth, on the site of today's Hanworth Air Park. To Whitehead's delight, a new order to build Sopwith Pups followed. He felt that this gave his firm credibility as the Pup was proving effective in front line service.

The first test pilot, Herbert Sykes, arrived in his own Martinsyde two-seat biplane which he kept on the airfield. When he was injured in a test-flight crash on 26 June, his place was at taken by Captain A. Payze from the RFC.

But Whitehead was as good at spending money as he was generating sales, and unfortunately his expenditure soon started to outstrip the incoming cash. Perhaps he thought production would continue at its current levels indefinitely. The standard payment for a Pup less engine and Vickers machine gun was around £700 and by June 1917 the factory was producing one Pup a day, but his monthly wage bill was now £11,000. The factory could not continue by building aircraft under licence alone. Although Whitehead tried to design their own aircraft, they kept coming up against the fact that either the other manufacturers were winning the contracts or the designs he produced were simply not needed.

At the end of the war the Ministry of Munitions began operating a phased run-down scheme to try to avoid large layoffs of labour and bankruptcy. But these reduced contracts were not going to satisfy a lavish spender like Whitehead. Up to 1 September 1918 a profit had been made of £19,686, but it was soon swallowed up in promoting new schemes for peace-time aviation. Hanworth was promoted by Whitehead as the London Airport of the future, and he even forecast commuting by aeroplane. Flying across the Atlantic might have saved Whitehead's cause, but in 1919 his company became so financially hobbled that it crashed.

The Alliance 'Atlantic' was the Alliance Aeroplane Co. entry that was completed too late to contest the prize. (*Flight*)

ALLIANCE AEROPLANE CO

The Alliance-Napier P2 *Seabird* was the only entrant scheduled to be flown by its designer J.A. Peters with Captain W.R. Curtiss navigating. The aircraft was designed as a long-range biplane with a crew of two housed in an enclosed cockpit. The engine was a single Napier 'Lion' producing 450hp. Although J.A. Peters paid the £100 entrance fee to compete for the Daily Mail Atlantic prize, the aircraft was not completed in time so the team never made it to Newfoundland. However, *Seabird* did achieve some fame when it was flown non-stop from London to Madrid in just under eight hours on 31 July 1919. A second Seabird was built to compete for the £10,000 prize put up by the Australian government for the first flight to Australia. The aircraft took off on 19 November 1919 but crashed soon afterwards over Surbiton killing both crew. The company failed to recover from the tragedy and closed its doors in 1920.

BOULTON & PAUL

During the war, Boulton and Paul built up a formidable reputation building aircraft under licence from its Norwich factory. The company had produced three prototypes of its P.7 Bourges bomber but the lack of orders saw the project go no further. However, like other manufacturers, Boulton & Paul saw opportunities in entering the transatlantic challenge. As a result, the first P.7 prototype was 'cannibalised' to provide the first of two P.8s which were to be used to mount their challenge. The P8 was a twin-engine biplane with an enclosed cockpit. Powered by two Napier 'Lion' engines, it entered with a cruising speed of around 120 mph. The aircraft was originally designed as a transport with passengers housed in an enclosed and roomy cabin. The pilot was the only person outside although he was protected from the elements by a large windscreen. For the Atlantic challenge the cabin was to be used chiefly for housing the extra fuel tanks necessary for the crossing. Six tanks were installed giving the aircraft a range of around 3,000 miles in good weather –

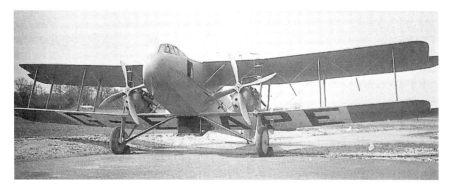

Following the failure to win the transatlantic prize, Boulton & Paul attempted to market the P.8 as a civilian airliner but with little success. (*Flight*)

Boulton & Paul had planned to enter 2 aircraft and the team's representative arrived in St John's on the very same the day that Alcock & Brown took off. (*Flight*)

the engines could be run at half power once up to cruising speed. The intention was to take two machines over to Newfoundland and make the crossing with a crew of three: Major K.S. Savory, pilot, Captain J.H. Woolmer, navigator, and Captain A.L. Howarth as observer. The aircraft had a unique feature: a device in the floor by the pilot's feet which could lock the wing flaps and elevators in any position. At the same time, the rudder control could be changed over from the rudder bar to the wheel which ordinarily operated the ailerons. The thinking behind this was to relieve the pilot's workload on such a long flight as he would be simply steering the aircraft with the wheel like a car. Boulton and Paul's designer, J.D. North, claimed that as the aircraft was very stable, all the pilot would have to do was keep her on course. Unfortunately, the aircraft was damaged beyond repair in a take-off accident and a second machine could not be completed in time to take part. With spectacular bad timing, their representative arrived in Newfoundland the very day that Alcock and Brown took off at the start of their historic flight.

FELIXSTOWE FURY

John Cyril Porte's interest in aviation had begun when he was serving in the Royal Navy but it was not until he was medically discharged that he took his interest further and learned to fly. But, following a meeting with the American aircraft pioneer Glenn Curtiss, Porte moved to America. There he worked with Curtiss in developing aircraft that could take off and land on water. It was Porte's idea to add a notch in the hull to enable the aircraft to lift off from water more easily. On hearing of the *Daily Mail*'s transatlantic challenge, Curtiss and Porte were commissioned by department store magnate Rodman Wanamaker to design and build a large, twin-engine flying boat capable of crossing the Atlantic. The aircraft was a conventional biplane design with two-bay, unstaggered wings of unequal span, with two tractor engines mounted side by side above the fuselage in the gap between the wings. Wingtip pontoons were attached directly below the lower wings near their tips. The aircraft resembled Curtiss's earlier flying boat designs but was considerably larger, and was designed to carry enough fuel to cover 1,100 miles. The three crew members were accommodated in a fully enclosed cabin. Named *America* and launched 22 June 1914, trials began the following day and soon revealed a serious shortcoming in the design: the tendency for the nose of the aircraft to try to submerge as engine power increased while taxiing on water. This phenomenon had not been encountered before, since Curtiss's earlier designs had not used such powerful engines. To counteract this effect,

Curtiss fitted fins to the sides of the bow to add hydrodynamic lift, but soon replaced these with sponsons to add buoyancy. Both prototypes, once fitted with sponsons, were then called Model H-2s. These sponsons would remain a prominent feature of flying boat hull design in the decades to follow. With the problem resolved, preparations for the transatlantic crossing resumed, and 5 August 1914 was selected to take advantage of the full moon.

These plans were interrupted by the outbreak of the First World War, which also saw Porte, who was to pilot the *America* with George Hallett, recalled to service with the Royal Navy. Impressed by the capabilities he had witnessed, Porte urged the Admiralty to commandeer (and later purchase) the *America* and her sister aircraft from Curtiss. By the late summer of 1914 they were both successfully fully tested and shipped to England on 30 September, aboard RMS *Mauretania*. This was followed by a decision to order a further twelve similar aircraft, one Model H-2 and the remaining Model H-4s, four examples of the latter actually being assembled in the UK by Saunders. All of these were essentially identical to the design of the *America*, and indeed were all referred to as 'Americas' in Royal Navy service. This initial batch was followed by an order for another fifty.

The 'H' Series aircraft evolved into the 'Felixstowe' series of flying boats culminating in the Felixstowe 'Fury'. Started in early 1917, the Porte Super-baby was a huge aircraft by the standards of the time, with a

The Felixstowe Fury's departure was delayed as a large enough ship to ferry the enormous aircraft could not be found. The Fury was later destroyed in a fatal crash.

wingspan comparable to the monoplane flying-boat designs of the 1930s. The hull, considered the best of all Porte's designs, was planked diagonally with cedar wood, forming a very wide, slightly concave 'V'-shaped bottom whereas previous Felixstowe models had used a straight-edged section. Experiments on the effect of different steps in the hull were carried out on a model in the Froude tank at the National Physical Laboratory, first with one, then two and three, finally reverting to two steps.

Powered by five Rolls-Royce Eagle VIII engines, the 'Fury' first flew on 24 April 1919. Flight testing went well including carrying out seven-hour flights. An Atlantic crossing seemed well within the aircraft's capabilities and plans were made to ship it to Cape Broyle in Newfoundland to join the other teams. But the aircraft was so large that no ship could be found with a large enough capacity to transport it over. Also the Air Ministry was unwilling to provide funding and so the project was abandoned in the third week of May.

FAIREY

Fairey was another British manufacturer which had produced a number of successful aircraft during the war. One of its most successful designs

was the Fairey III, versions of which saw service as both landplane and seaplane. For the Atlantic challenge it was decided to enter a modified IIIC seaplane variant powered by a single Rolls-Royce Eagle VIII engine. Its pilot was Australian Sydney Pickles who was well-known as a pre-war pioneer but had also served as a pilot in the Royal Naval Air Service at the start of

Sydney Pickles was due to fly Fairey Aviation Co's entry. He was one of the few who survived those early, pioneering years of flight. He died in 1975 in Canada after a long career in aviation. (Library of Congress)

the war before becoming a flying instructor. His navigator was Captain A.G.D. West. The Fairey entry was one of only two seaplanes and testing was going well until Alcock and Brown made their successful crossing. After that there seemed little point in continuing and the project was scrapped.

HANDLEY PAGE

Handley Page's entry was the largest aircraft flying in the world. The Handley Page V/1500 was based on the earlier O/100 and O/400 bombers as a long range heavy bomber which could reach Berlin from airfields in East Anglia. To make this possible it was fitted with four Rolls-Royce Eagle VIII engines configured with two facing forwards and two rearwards. But the aircraft never saw operational service against Germany as the Armistice was declared just as three aircraft were about to taxi out on their first bombing mission. For the Atlantic attempt it was expected to weigh 32,000lbs when fully laden. Amongst the kit was a self-inflating balloon which could be released in emergency to attract the attention of passing ships. With all the kit and the weight of 1,700 gallons of fuel, the Handley Page needed at least half a mile for take-off.

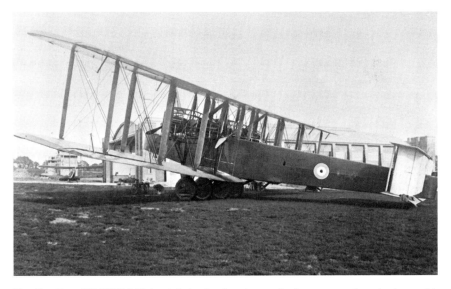

Handley Page HP V1500 'Atlantic'. At the time it was the largest aeroplane in the world. (A Flying History)

Handley Page team in front of their V1500 'Atlantic'. (A Flying History)

Locals described the crates carrying the Handley Page aircraft as being as big as houses. (A Flying History)

The team was headed by Admiral Mark Kerr, the first Royal Navy flag officer to learn to fly, who acted as manager and assistant pilot. The pilot was Major Herbert Brackley who had been taught to fly by Alcock while he was instructing at the Royal Naval Air Service school at Eastchurch on the Isle of Sheppey. The wireless operator was Frederick Wyatt, and the navigator, Tryggve Gran who was the first to fly across the North Sea and had been a member of the expedition that discovered the remains of Scott and his companions who had failed in their attempt to be the first to reach the South Pole.

When the aircraft was dismantled for shipment to Newfoundland, it filled over one hundred crates; some were said by the local inhabitants to be the size of houses. The crates then had to be hauled to Harbour Grace where the aircraft was to be assembled.

SHORT BROS

Handley Page had not even set off for Newfoundland when the Short Brothers declared themselves ready to make their attempt as soon as the weather would let them. Unlike all the other entrants they were going to fly from east to west. Although this was against the prevailing winds, it was going to save them weeks in shipping the aircraft over to Newfoundland.

Short Brothers was the world's first manufacturer to build volume production of an aircraft design from their base on the Isle of Sheppey. Throughout the war the company designed and built a long series of successful floatplanes for the Royal Naval Air Service.

Their entry for the race was based on the Short Shirl which had been designed as a torpedo bomber capable of carrying the navy's largest torpedo. As landing back on an aircraft carrier deck was still not possible, the Shirl had floatation bags to keep it on the water's surface until it could be lifted back onto a ship. For the race, the Shirl was given longer wings requiring a third set of struts. The fuselage was modified to take a second seat for the navigator configured so that he would be sitting almost beside the pilot. The space for the torpedo was filled with a large petrol tank which, in the event of ditching into the sea, could be drained quickly to provide additional floatation. The extra fuel gave the Shirl a range of around 3,200 miles in quiet air which would have been more than adequate for an Atlantic crossing even if the prevailing winds were unhelpful.

Above: The Short 'Shamrock' was based on the Short 'Shirl' torpedo bomber. An extra fuel tank replaced the torpedo. (A Flying History)

Left: Major J.C.P. Wood was in the RNAS before being chosen to pilot the Short Bros 'Shamrock'. (Library of Congress)

Capt. C.C. Wylie, navigator for the Shorts Shamrock attempt flying east to west. (Library of Congress)

Their plan was to fly to Limerick in Ireland and launch their attempt from there. The aircraft was to be flown by pilot Major J.C.P. Wood, a veteran of the First World War with more than 1,000 hours flying experience to his name, assisted by his navigator, Captain C.C. Wyllie.

VICKERS

The last manufacturer to enter was Vickers. The company had been unsure about submitting an entry because of the risk but their newly appointed test pilot, John Alcock, convinced Maxwell Muller, works manager at Weybridge, that not only should Vickers enter but that he had the right experience of long distance flying at night to give the project its greatest chance of success. What's more, he argued, they had the right aircraft for the flight, the F27 Vimy.

Alcock talked to Muller about the hours spent as a prisoner of war thinking about how he might make the flight. His enthusiasm was infectious, and he clearly knew what he was talking about. It was enough to convince Muller they could do it and the project was given the 'green light'.

The aircraft Alcock was to use was a Vickers Vimy Mark IV powered by two Rolls Royce Eagle engines. Like the Handley Page entry, the Vimy was designed as a long-range bomber but had entered service too late to see active service. Vickers' chief designer Reginald 'Rex' Pearson worked quickly once the Air Board had agreed the specification for a long-range bomber that could carry twelve bombs and a crew of three. Designated the FB 27, design to the production of three prototypes took just four months. However as Rolls Royce was unable to produce enough Eagle engines to meet demand, the first prototype was powered by the more readily available Hispano-Suiza engines.

The first protype made its first flight on 30 November 1917 from Royal Flying Corps Station Joyce Green in Kent piloted by Captain Gordon Bell. It was then sent up to Martlesham Heath in Suffolk to begin trials. The FB 27 performed exceptionally well as it could take off with a greater payload than its main rival, the Handley Page O/400 which had around twice the effective engine power. But the Hispano-Suiza engines were proving too unreliable and so the aircraft was sent back to the factory where it was fitted with an all-new Salmson water-cooled aero engine.

The second prototype was given new wings and ailerons and powered by a pair of Sunbeam Maori engines which also proved unreliable. Indeed this aircraft crashed due to engine failure during testing at Martlesham Heath. The third prototype, fitted with Fiat A-12 bis engines, fared little better. A stall induced by the pilot resulted in a hard landing – hard enough to detonate the bombload, killing the pilot and destroying the aircraft.

The third Vimy prototype with Fiat A.12 Engines. This aircraft was destroyed when a bomb load detonated following a hard landing. (BAE Systems)

RAF version of the Vimy bomber. (BAE Systems)

Despite these setbacks, a fourth prototype was built to try out the Rolls-Royce Eagle VIII engines. The new aircraft had been given an enlarged tail unit and it also had a greatly enlarged fuel capacity. Otherwise, it was more or less the same as the previous aircraft. Testing began on 11 October 1918, even though the Vimy was now in production. It was called the Vimy after the Battle of Vimy Ridge of April 1917. It was perhaps a propitious choice of name as the battle was fought by Canadian forces. Today it is the location of the Canadian National Vimy Memorial commemorating the Canadians' achievement and sacrifice.

Over 1,000 aircraft were ordered under wartime contracts but in the confusion of cancelled orders and unfinished aircraft following the Armistice, the total actually delivered is still uncertain, although it appears to have been in excess of 230, with 147 built by Vickers at its Weybridge, Crayford and Bexleyheath factories. The rest were built under licence.

The Vimy selected to make the Atlantic crossing was the Mark IV version powered by Rolls-Royce Eagle VIII engines each producing 350hp. Extra fuel tanks were added taking its capacity to 865 gallons as well as 50 gallons of oil. It now had a range of 2,440 miles and a top speed of 100mph. Additional weight was saved by removing the bomb racks and all other military hardware. The main alteration to the fuselage was the

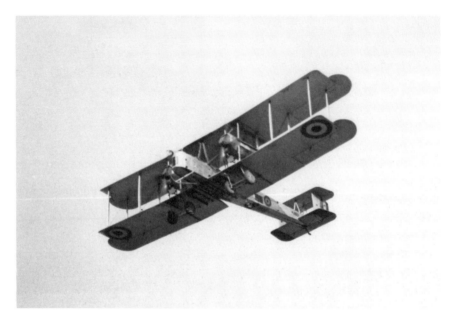

An RAF Vimy. The Vimy remained in RAF service until 1938 when they were being used for searchlight practice. (BAE Systems)

The Vimy under construction at Vickers' factory at Weybridge. (BAE Systems)

The Vimy before being dismantled for shipping to Newfoundland. (BAE Systems)

widening of the cockpit so that pilot and navigator could sit side by side for better communications, although once dressed in bulky flying kit, the cockpit space was going to be cramped. The observer's cockpit at the front of the fuselage was hidden under a streamlined covering and occupied by yet another fuel tank. Apart from these small modifications it was a standard Vimy straight off the production line at Weybridge. The Vimy was the thirteenth aircraft to be made but the number thirteen was Alcock's lucky number. Alcock followed the production of his aircraft in great detail so that he would be in a better position to oversee the reassembly once they got to Newfoundland.

It was while he was at Weybridge that he had a chance introduction to the man who was to share his destiny, Arthur Whitten Brown.

With the Armistice came unemployment for Brown and it was while looking for work that he found himself in Maxwell Muller's office at Vickers' Brooklands factory. The topic of navigation came up and it dawned on Muller that Brown might be a suitable navigator for Alcock. As luck would have it, Alcock was in the factory and when the two met; it became clear that they shared a dream and that Brown was indeed the right man.

The two men complemented each other well. Alcock was quite a solid man, described in an article as someone who would be 'a comforting

The Alcock & Brown Vimy had the nose skid removed and the forward observer's cockpit covered over. (BAE Systems)

Inside the cockpit showing the Vimy's very basic controls. (BAE Systems)

Alcock and Brown stand by their Vimy. (BAE Systems)

companion in a street or music hall row'. In temperament he was anything but ill-tempered which was just as well as his easy charm would be much needed once they got to St John's. Brown was the quieter of the two.

As the airframe came together, Alcock was leaving nothing to chance. He even visited the Rolls-Royce factory at Derby to watch the actual engines he would use being given a test run. Rolls-Royce also assigned engineer Bob Lyons to accompany the Vickers team.

By mid-April 1919 the Vimy was ready for its first flight. On Good Friday, the same day that Shorts started their ill-fated east to west attempt, they gave the Vimy a thorough test flight, which it passed with flying colours. Indeed it was so successful that the aircraft was dismantled and packed ready for immediate shipment to St John's. Unfortunately there were strikes and time was lost as the precious cargo was delayed at the London Docks. It was not until 13 May that the SS *Glendevon* eventually left for Newfoundland with ten Vickers support crew including Bob Dicker, whose role was to oversee the machine's assembly, carpenter Ernie Pitman, and of course Bob Lyons from Rolls-Royce.

By now the Martinsyde and Sopwith teams had been in Newfoundland for weeks and were ready to make their attempt. Rumour had it they would try on 16 April, two days before Alcock and Brown had even flown their Vimy. But bad weather closed in and so Hawker, Mackenzie-Grieve, Raynham and Morgan had to kick their heels a while longer. To add to the pressure, the Handley Page aircraft had left on 15 April. Alcock and Brown

Transatlantic Vimy, Newfoundland - Chick. Unknown. Sid Davies. Montgomery. Unknown. Jack Westcott. Potter. Harry Crouch. Frank Waud. Unknown. Pitman. (BAE Systems)

had much catching up to do if they were to stand a chance. On 4 May they set sail on the *Mauretania* from Southampton bound for Halifax, Nova Scotia. The journey was a great opportunity for Brown to put some of his navigation theories into practice as the *Mauretania*'s commander, Captain Rostron, gave him free rein on the bridge as well as passing on some useful advice. Up to now, everything he knew about navigation was what he had learned from books, and he had his own being ideas as to how this might be applied across nearly 2,000 miles, most of it being the Atlantic. He would only get one chance to get it right and time was not on their side.

THE US NAVY

As the *Mauretania* steamed her way across the North Atlantic, the US Navy was about to launch its attempt at an Atlantic crossing using flying boats designed by Glenn Curtiss. The one major change in the rules for the *Daily Mail* competition was that no stopping was allowed: the flight had to be non-stop. This did not matter to the US Navy as they were entering for the prestige, besides which, as employees of the US government, the crews would not have been allowed to accept the prize money.

The US Navy originally wanted a long-distance aircraft to counter the threat of German submarines attacking Allied shipping. During the war, flying boats underwent a dramatic improvement in their performance, range and armament, but for aircraft to have real potential as anti-submarine weapons they would need to be able to fly from the United States to Europe. Aviation pioneer Glenn Curtiss was given the contract to come up with a design for such an aircraft, which he did in just three days.

The design that went through to production used three Liberty engines in a tractor configuration and one centre-mounted motor facing backwards to help push the aircraft along. The design featured a relatively short hull made of spruce and measured 43 feet although the overall length of the aircraft was just over 68 feet. The tail section was raised so that it would sit up over waves. There were also small pontoons under the wings to provide additional lateral stability.

The aircraft were designated NC, the N for Navy and C for Curtiss, and on 4 October 1917 NC-1 taxied out for her maiden flight. Commander Richardson was at the controls and after a series of taxiing manoeuvres, he managed a short hop followed by a proper flight.

Commander Jerome C. Hunsaker, one of the project team who ran the programme, later described what it was like flying these large aircraft:

> The big boats had dual controls and the two aviators sat side by side and worked together on the controls which required strong effort at times. Read was a relatively small man, and he chose Stone because of his size and strength. The two were a good team. Stone had experience with flying boats, which were notoriously difficult to keep from stalling in rough air or at reduced speed. Stone also had experience in bad visibility weather. Stone had been a test pilot and knew how the crude instruments of the day could give indications contrary to the reliable 'seat of the pants' signals of acceleration. On the eighteen-hour flight of the NC-4 to the Azores, Read's function as a navigator required him to stand in the forward cockpit. Stone was in fact the chief aviator with Lt Walter Hinton sitting beside him as a partner.

But the Armistice on 11 November 1918 put further development on hold until a group of officers managed to persuade their superiors to sanction an official attempt to demonstrate the navy's flying capability.

The NC-4 that made the successful crossing from the Azores to Lisbon and then on to Plymouth. (Library of Congress)

The plan was for four NCs to make the attempt but the whole Atlantic programme nearly ended before it had even started when NC-2 crashed on a trials flight. Then, on 4 May, a fire damaged NC-1 and NC-4. The decision was taken to repair the two using parts of NC-2. Four days later, they were ready to begin their epic journey beginning with a positioning flight to Newfoundland.

ST JOHN'S

It was in the early hours of the morning of 13 May that Alcock and Brown left the warmth of their carriage and stepped out into a cold wet St John's morning. The gloom of their surroundings was in sharp contrast to the late spring weather they had left behind in England ten days earlier. Snow still lay on the ground and the rain seemed relentless. As they stretched tired limbs there was a moment to reflect on the journey from Port aux Basques on the narrow-gauge Reid Railway that had taken forty hours instead of the scheduled twenty-seven. Their first stop was to find rooms at the Cochrane Hotel which had become something of an unofficial headquarters for the teams hoping to make the transatlantic crossing. There were also a number of journalists staying, waiting to file what would almost certainly be the biggest story of the year. There they found the welcoming hospitality of Agnes Dooley, who every morning would make sure the Atlantic flyers were provisioned with sandwiches and fresh coffee just in case 'today was the day'. There were old friends staying there too: Raynham, Morgan, Hawker and Mackenzie-Grieve knew each other from the pre-war years. Hawker, Raynham and Alcock had competed against one another in numerous flying events and although they may have been rivals for the great prize there was also a camaraderie that saw them through the bad times and setbacks.

For Alcock and Brown there was little time for resting as they were the last to enter the race and had a lot of catching up to do if they were to even stand a chance. Their first task was to find a suitable airfield from which to operate. As Brown wryly observed, 'even its best friends cannot claim that it is ideal for aviation.' He went on to describe it:

> The whole of the island has no ground that might be made into a first-class aerodrome. The district around St John's is especially difficult. Some of the country is wooded, but for the most part it shows a rolling, switchback surface, across which aeroplanes cannot taxi with any degree of smoothness. The soil is soft and dotted with boulders, for only a light layer of it covers the rock stratum. Another handicap is the prevalence of thick fogs, which roll westward from the sea.

The bad weather had to a point helped the team from Vickers as their opposition had been in St John's for many weeks but had not been able to fly due to poor weather. Indeed there were dark mutterings that 'someone' was trying to sabotage the whole thing by feeding in false weather forecasts. The situation was only made worse by increasingly agitated cables from the UK wanting to know why on earth they had not yet launched when the weather seemed to be fine their side of the ocean?

Hawker and Grieve, along with an engineer from Rolls-Royce and a newsreel cameraman from Jurys Imperial Pictures, left England in the *Digby* on 20 March, with their machine carefully packed into two big crates and a few small cases. But when they arrived in St John's, they found it packed by Arctic ice and so they had to sail round to Placentia Bay, arriving on the 28th. As the harbour was too shallow for the *Digby* they had to transfer all the boxes across to a smaller vessel, the *Portia*, to take them ashore. It was then a case of manhandling all their luggage onto the narrow-gauge railway which took them back to St John's.

Lt Clements' weather forecasts played a critical role in the outcome of the race.

Captain Montague Fenn and his ground staff had gone over previously and had already chosen an airfield at Mount Pearl to the southwest of St John's aerodrome. He had also made sure that an excellent wooden shed was erected before they arrived. This was built of rough timber but was greatly preferable to the tent which had been taken over in case of need, as the weather was very bad, and despite being late spring, the whole place was under snow. This had made choosing an airfield very difficult, but Captain Fenn got the best place available. Hawker was not the last to observe: 'The many excellent friends we made in Newfoundland will not accuse me of slighting their hospitable country when I say that it is the last place in which one would look for spacious landing grounds.'

Of course they knew this pretty well from maps before they started, but if anything the maps seemed to flatter the country, and actually, from the aerodrome point of view, it was a little worse than Hawker had expected. All along he had realised that the aerodrome difficulty would probably be the worst thing they would have to contend with. To start with, the nature of the country made it probable that they would not get much smooth ground in one patch, and, secondly, it was necessary to make several trial flights before setting off on their Atlantic attempt. Therefore they would be dependent on wind direction to make test flights. They certainly could not afford to risk damaging the aeroplane by attempting trial flights under bad conditions. It was because of the constant bad weather that it was impossible for them to thoroughly test the second wireless set in the air which had been sent out to them. Between its arrival and their start there was not a day on which they could make a flight and know that they could make a safe landing.

The airfield was about 450 feet above sea level and seemed to catch all the sorts of winds they did not want. It was an L-shaped piece of ground about 400 yards on its longest limb, and about 200 yards along the shorter. The long part of the 'L' faced roughly east-west and the short part north-south, the latter being at the eastern end. The L shape was due to the fact that the ground skirted a hill about 200 feet high with rather steep sides. The ground had long been under snow, and it came as no surprise that it was completely devoid of drainage. The short limb was straight uphill from the south, at which end it had high trees, there were also low trees at each end of the long limb. It was acceptable for starting in a due east wind, though in these circumstances they had to start off from soft and boggy ground. This was potentially dangerous if the aircraft started to sink into the ground. With a west wind they faced finishing their run in the soft ground and would also be running uphill. The soft ground was less of a problem if the aircraft was lightly loaded, but for the Atlantic crossing it was going to be loaded to its maximum with precious little margin for a lengthy take-off. The risk was enormous, and they would have to be very careful indeed.

The problems of the soft ground could be slightly relieved by filling with stone and Captain Fenn had already planned for this, but the airfield was about six miles from St John's, which made finding the labour and then transporting the materials quite difficult. At one time they had a gang of about sixty men busily filling up the worst of the soft areas. Needless to say, any sort of take-off was impossible when the ground was covered with snow.

Most of the trial flights of the aeroplane back at Brooklands had been made with a four-bladed propeller. But it was decided in Newfoundland to use the two-bladed propeller which they had taken with them, as this gave a little more thrust even though it meant a small reduction in speed. If the aircraft could not get off the ground at the start of the journey, then there would be no crossing at all.

The original intention when Hawker and the team left England was, if possible, to get away before anyone else arrived in Newfoundland. But they soon realised that this plan was out of the question on account not only of unfavourable winds, but also because of the softness of the airfield, made worse by heavy snowfalls. There was no choice but to sit and wait.

Waiting for a suitable weather window tested their patience to the limit. Despite the hospitality of their hosts, St John's was a small town then and so there was very little to keep minds occupied during the enforced periods of idleness. Inevitably, tempers sometimes frayed.

But there were jobs to be done even if they only occupied the team for a few hours. Every day they would go up to the airfield in a car, which sometimes provided amusement by getting stuck in snow-drifts from which it had to be dug out. Then there was always some fine tuning to be done on the machine – imagined or otherwise. It was also necessary to run the engine up to see that all was well, the wireless set experimented with, and the water emptied in and out of the cooling system to prevent any chance of the engine freezing. However, it appears that neither Hawker nor the rest of the team noticed that deposits were forming in the system. It was this oversight that was identified as the probable cause of their engine failure and the end of their attempt on the crossing.

The aircraft had taken about a week to assemble, and at any time after that they were always ready to go. All they needed was just enough time to get the tanks filled up, the all-important mail aboard, thermos flasks filled, and the engine nicely warmed up. The aircraft had already had its official Royal Aero Club seal attached, so all they could do was wait.

The weather-induced delay gave Hawker and Mackenzie Grieve an opportunity to test their survival equipment. A unique feature of the Sopwith was the detachable boat that formed part of the top fuselage. Practising launching it in a lake was one thing, but how would they fare in a mid-Atlantic swell? Their time on the water also gave them the opportunity to test out their survival suits. Like the immersion suits worn by sailors and pilots today, these provided a tight seal at the neck and wrists. The lining was filled with kapok although this was replaced with air bags which could by inflated by mouth. According to Hawker the suits performed well, although pulling themselves out of the confines of a cockpit in an aircraft that was sinking into the ocean would be an altogether different prospect.

The tedium of their daily routine was interrupted when Freddie Raynham and Major C.W.F. Morgan arrived at St John's on 10 April with their Martinsyde *Raymor*. A Martinsyde representative had been out to Newfoundland even before Hawker and the rest of the Sopwith team and had secured what they considered the best landing ground in a meadow by

Quidi Vidi lake. Hawker was not convinced they had the best as he observed that it was very narrow and only really suitable for taking off in a south-westerly or westerly wind. But the weather was eroding any advantage Hawker had in being first to be ready to fly.

Raynham and Morgan and their team had soon finished assembling their *Raymor*, resplendent in its red and yellow colour scheme, but the weather was preventing them from making enough test flights.

Freddie Raynham was an old friend of Hawker's from before the war and so they were grateful for the new company. They were all staying at the same hotel, the Cochrane, where they passed the time playing practical jokes on each other, visiting the local weather station together, and just finding any number of ways of keeping themselves occupied. But, of course, they were going to be competing against one another and so they watched each other like cats watch mice. If the waiting was stressful, then this only added to the pressure. In the end they recognised that the tension between them was not going to help their cause, or that of the greater goal of doing their best for British aviation, so they arrived at a compromise: each would give the other a couple of hours' notice before starting. They would also notify the wireless stations, who in turn would have time to send warnings out to ships on or near their route. As Hawker saw it, as their aircraft were of similar performance, they would be able to keep each other company and provide mutual support if necessary, for at least part of the way.

Although reaching an understanding helped relieve the tension, the weather did not help. Sometimes it would clear up a bit and look promising, but the reports from the meteorological station almost always continued to put a different complexion on it. The thick white fogs would, whenever the wind went into the east, roll in from the Grand Banks that lie just off Newfoundland's south-east coast, and smother them. Sometimes they had to fight the urge to have a go in spite of them, but their airfields were not the sort of ground that could be landed on in poor visibility.

But if the weekly report carried in 24 April's edition of *Flight* magazine was anything to go by, the competition was hotting up. The number of entries was up to nine with the Alliance Aeroplane Company being the latest entry.

Boulton and Paul were working night and day at their Norwich factory to get two aircraft ready and had sent a representative to St John's to look for a suitable airfield.

The same article reported that the Handley Page aircraft was on its way although they would not make an attempt at a crossing until mid-May, and even then only in the most ideal of conditions. Work was already underway at Harbour Grace where they expected to clear a runway of not less than half a mile in length although a full mile was preferable. There were reports of the imminent arrival of the Whitehead machine and one of the Felixstowe Furies was on its way as well. It was reported that Captain A.G.D. West had been appointed as navigator and reserve pilot to Sydney Pickles in the Fairey entry. Ominously, it carried news that the US Navy would mount an attempt in May to fly across the Atlantic non-stop in one of their Glen Curtiss designed NC flying boats. A team of mechanics and engineers had already left Long Island on the *Aroostook* bound for Newfoundland. It was understood that the *Aroostook* would then head for the Azores and act as a supply ship. The cruisers *Baltimore* and *Columbia* had also been detailed to provide support for the attempt.

On 17 April Freddy Raynham made a successful test flight lasting over an hour. He now felt as confident as he could be that he was now ready. Trial weather balloons had been sent up to see if there were better conditions at higher altitude, but they were disappearing into the mist at 6,000 feet. If the weather did not improve soon and allow Hawker to get away, the skies over Newfoundland were going to be very busy. Public interest in the race was mounting by the day as a steady stream of stories came in from reporters in Newfoundland. There was no detail unworthy of their attention.

But the big story of the week was the failed attempt by the Short Brothers' entry to fly from east to west. Shorts were the only team to go against the conventional 'wisdom' that believed prevailing winds favoured a west to east crossing. Oswald Short argued that as wind direction and strength changes at different altitudes, how could people be certain that west to east was better as nobody had yet flown the route to prove the theory. Either way, the spring weather in England was proving as fickle as it was in Newfoundland.

Through the first week of April, reports from England suggested that preliminary trials on the Short Brothers *Shamrock* had gone well and that they were ready. However, true to form, the weather throughout the month had been varied but generally poor. But, on the 18th, the team at Shorts were met with warm sunny weather. On Good Friday afternoon – 19 April 1919 – they were confident enough to begin their journey. Taking off from Eastchurch on the Isle of Sheppey their plan was to fly first to Ireland.

Four hours into the flight and all was going well as they flew over Holyhead on the coast of North Wales and set a course for Dublin where a large crowd waited to greet Major Wood and Captain Wylie.

They climbed to 3,000 ft as the Welsh coast slid behind them. But then their luck ran out. Twelve miles out to sea the *Shamrock*'s engine coughed

The Martinsyde 'Raymor' taxies along by Quidi Vidi lake.

and spluttered before cutting out completely, due, it was subsequently found, to an airlock in the fuel system. The two pilots could not get it started, and so with no alternative they turned back for the shore. But they were too far out for the *Shamrock* to glide to the coast and so they set down on the water. As they did so, the machine flipped over leaving Wood and Wyllie to sit on the upturned aircraft's axle and await rescue.

53

The aircraft was towed back to shore and loaded onto a lorry for transport back to Rochester, as they thought it could be repaired and ready for another attempt later in the year – Major Wood thought it could be restored within a couple of weeks. But it turned out that the aircraft was more badly damaged than was first thought and could not be repaired before being overtaken by events in Newfoundland. The decision was taken to abandon any further attempts to cross the Atlantic from east to west. In fact, the first heavier than air flight was only achieved in 1928.

The weather continued to occupy the aviators' attention. Despite the country being buried under a blanket of heavy snow in the last week of April, England in May was much drier than normal. An expectant public were greeted by a succession of warm, sunny days making it difficult for them to understand why, out in the mid-Atlantic, and on or near a straight line drawn on the map between St John's and Brooklands, 'south-westerly depressions' and similar meteorological 'details' were preventing Hawker and Grieve from taking to the air.

Everyone was tired with waiting. Day after day the reporters gathered at St John's were running out of stories to report. Dark rumours began to circulate of sabotage – that the favourable weather reports from England were somehow being 'doctored' to paint a less inviting picture. It was reported that the Air Ministry had taken steps to prevent any interference with the official meteorological intelligence service and that henceforth reports would be transmitted to the navigators in code. The bad weather was all the more frustrating because the sun seemed to be shining everywhere else in the world. Mackenzie Grieve received a message from the women in the cable office of the British War Mission in New York:

> SIR, DO BUCK UP AND START. WE
> CANNOT STAND THE SUSPENSE
> MUCH LONGER. BEST OF LUCK
> FROM TWO CABLETTES.

Of course, Hawker and Raynham were ready to go at a moment's notice. Final details had been arranged, such as how they would signal that they had crossed the Irish coast. Hawker decided that he would write the time of reaching the coast on the back of his charts and then throw them overboard with a message that whoever found them was to forward them to the Royal Aero Club in London. Raynham decided to use message bags with streamers. Morgan was to write messages as soon as the coast was crossed and throw them overboard as well.

The small community gathered in the Cochrane were given a jolt when on 8 May they got news that the flying boats of the US Navy had left their base at Far Rockaway on Long Island at 10 am that morning at the start of their thousand-mile journey to Newfoundland. They were heading for Trepassey Bay on Newfoundland's southern coast via Halifax. With little fanfare from the press and the outside world the engines of the three aircraft roared into life. The three of them, numbered NC-1, NC-3 and NC-4, taxied out and began their take-off runs. The flight to Newfoundland was a repositioning flight so they were ordered not to take any risks. NC-4 had only flown once before and so the leg to Halifax was to be a 'shakedown' flight.

Cape Cod passed below them as the three flying boats headed out over open sea, but all was not well in NC-4. The pusher engine in the middle had developed an oil leak. Lieutenant Commander Read had no alternative but to shut that engine down. It was not a major disaster as he knew the aircraft could fly well enough on three engines. At 2.05 pm they passed over the first 'station', the destroyer *McDermut*. They were well on course. But as they headed for the next destroyer the centre tractor engine seized. With two engines now out of commission, the crew on NC-4 faced little alternative but to put down on the open sea. A distress signal was sent out which both destroyers heard. Admiral Towers in NC-3 assumed the aircraft would land next to the *McDermut* for repairs and continued on his way. NC-4 altered course but the aircraft was losing altitude in poor visibility. However, with the water calm enough for a safe landing, Read directed NC-4 to be turned into the wind and a landing made. Once on the water they could not get through on the radio. Finding themselves in the open sea, eighty miles from the nearest land, they began to taxi towards Chatham Air Station, Massachusetts. For five hours they motored until, at dawn, just off the beach, they were spotted by two search aircraft. Within two days the bad engine was replaced and the other repaired. The only engine available at Chatham was a 300hp Liberty but it would have to do until the NC-4 reached Trepassey Bay where a 400hp engine was available. Unfortunately the weather turned really bad, with strong winds coming from the north-east. The prospect of forty knot headwinds meant a further delay, so NC-4 was unable to leave Chatham until the 14th.

Meanwhile, the NC-1 and NC-3 aircraft also ran into heavy weather en route. Buffeted by gusty winds it took the effort of both pilots to remain on course. They arrived at Halifax that day, but propeller problems delayed their departure until the 10th. They followed the line of 'station' ships, and as they passed Placentia Bay they sighted their first icebergs. The air remained

NC-1 and NC-3. (Library of Congress)

rough and it was now cold. At Trepassey Bay strong swells were running and the landings were made in strong gusty winds and an 'avalanche of spray'. By evening both aircraft were safely moored near the base ship USS *Aroostook*. The press holed up in St John's now had something to report on and were soon making the lengthy journey down to Trepassey Bay to see the big flying boats.

In the early hours of 13 May, John Alcock, Arthur Brown, and their party of eleven engineers arrived at the Cochrane Hotel. Although weary from their journey, they lost no time in beginning their search for a suitable landing ground. Hiring a car, they drove to Mount Pearl. It was the start of what was to be a long and difficult hunt for any kind of a field that could be improvised into an airfield. The uneven countryside through which they passed held out no hopes, and the company they met that evening at the Cochrane Hotel (Hawker, Grieve, Raynham, Morgan, and various officials and newspaper correspondents) were unanimous in declaring that the only suitable patches of ground had been appropriated and that they would find no others near St John's.

For about a week they continued the search for a landing ground. Tiring of hiring cars, they bought a second-hand Buick which registered 400

NC-1 at Trepassy, Newfoundland. (Library of Congress)

Many heavy crates containing the Vimy had to be dragged by horses from St John's to Quidi Vidi. (BAE Systems)

Some of the many
crates containing
the Vimy.
(BAE Systems)

57

miles at the time of purchase. Before long they were convinced that the speedometer must have been disconnected before the final 40,000 miles. The best possibilities for an airfield they could find were several level strips of meadowland, about 100 yards wide by 300 long, however, the Vimy fully loaded might need 500 yards of clear run into the wind. The only other fields they were able to locate were planted and the cost to purchase and destroy the crops would be prohibitive. Although their searches were turning up nothing but disappointment, the pacing out of fields provided good exercise. The Vimy was still at sea, but the poor weather was playing to their advantage as nobody could fly.

Evenings were mostly spent playing cards with the other competitors at the Cochrane Hotel, or in visits to the neighbouring film theatres. Their hosts in St John's were welcoming. The aviators explored the town pretty thoroughly and were soon able to recognize parts of it with their eyes closed and nostrils open, for its chief occupation appeared to be the drying of very dead cod.

Just before Alcock and Brown's arrival in St John's, the Handley Page team arrived in Harbour Grace on 10 May. Although it was a remote site,

Handley Page preparing their airfield at Harbour Grace. (A Flying History)

around sixty miles from St John's, it was probably the best airfield in Newfoundland at that moment. A reporter's description of the take-off strip showed just how difficult conditions were:

> It wasn't one field but a series of gardens and farms with rock walls between them. All of these had to be removed, as did three houses and a farm building. A heavy roller, drawn by three horses and weighed down with several hundred pounds of iron bars, eliminated the hummocks. The result, after a month, was a bumpy aerodrome.

Assembly of the giant Handley Page *Atlantic* began immediately, while Admiral Kerr enjoyed the hospitality of his host Robert Reid, the wealthy builder of Newfoundland's only railroad. The weather would improve eventually and then there would be a scramble to get going. Hawker in his Sopwith, Raynham in the Martinsyde, as well as the Handley Page effort and the Vickers team, all were hoping to win the *Daily Mail* prize as well as the honour of being the first to fly the Atlantic. The fact that the US Navy might be joining the competition only added to the tension.

What happened in the next few days was to have a profound effect on the outcome on the race. On the afternoon of 14 May, NC-4 left Chatham Air Station. However, rather than risk a night landing in Trepassey Bay, Lieutenant Commander Read decided to put in to Halifax. Besides, the centre engine was vibrating badly and the two outer motors were running

Handley Page preparing their airfield. (A Flying History)

Admiral Mark Kerr (CL), first senior naval officer to learn to fly and team leader with Herbert 'Brackles' Brackley (CR), pilot. (A Flying History)

Strong winds hampered the assembly of the enormous Handley Page V1500 'Atlantic'. (A Flying History)

Carpenters and riggers make sure the wings are correctly aligned. (A Flying History)

roughly as dirt had got into the carburettors. These problems were fixed on the morning of the 15th and NC-4 was airborne again by 1300 hours bound for Trepassey Bay.

Shortly after take-off the NC-4 received a message advising that the NC-1 and NC-3 aircraft would take off that afternoon, taking advantage of the full moon. But, as the NC-4 rounded Powell's Point they saw that the NC-1 and NC-3 had not departed yet. The problem was that although they had made several attempts to take off, neither aircraft would lift from the water. Lieutenant James Breese, an engineer on the NC-4, knew what the problem was. The fuel gauges on the NC had been calibrated while the aircraft was on land but now the aircraft had been moored in the harbour, the aircraft rode slightly nose down on the water so when a tank was filled to the full mark, they held a little over 200 pounds of additional fuel. Take-off weight was as critical to the NC-1 and NC-3 as it was to all the other aircraft gathered in Newfoundland and the American aircraft were simply too heavy for take-off. Departure was rescheduled for the following evening so that the aircraft would be approaching the Azores during daylight. This gave the crew of the NC-4 time to change the centre engine and test it in time for departure.

Although the American contingent were only in Trepassey for a few days, Alcock and Brown still found time to go down and see what was going on. On the 15th the flying boats were joined by an enormous airship, the C-5. Her crew had experienced a torrid time getting up to Trepassey Bay.

On 14 May the C-5 departed Montauk Point in clear weather. It made good time, but encountered heavy fog and thunderstorms near Saint Pierre Island and became lost for several hours. It eventually regained its way, but the extended trip caused the crew to exhaust its food supply and wind and rain continuously buffeted the blimp. The C-5 again became lost, this time over Newfoundland, when its radio navigation equipment malfunctioned. C-5's crew used its voice radio to contact the US Navy cruiser *Chicago*, which was in St John's, and the radio signal was used to guide C-5 to the tracks of the Colonial Railroad, which it followed to St John's and a safe landing at 11 am on 15 May. The commander of the blimp, Lieutenant Commander Coll, said it was the roughest trip he had ever experienced.

Most of the crew left to eat lunch and sleep, while the few remaining men began to service the blimp's engines. In the meantime a storm rolled in and additional cables were tied over the blimp to secure it. Additional crewmen from the *Chicago* were also brought in to help. The wind intensified from 30 to 40 miles per hour with even higher gusts. The wind strength was too much and the blimp began to break free from its additional cables. The engines couldn't be restarted because they were under maintenance, so Lieutenant Charles Little attempted to pull the emergency cord to open the gasbag and deflate it. But the cord broke and the C-5 began to lift off, tearing out the few remaining cables and injuring two crewmen as they sprang loose. Little was also injured when he decided to jump from the rising blimp. The C-5 was blown eastward, out over the Atlantic Ocean.

The destroyer USS *Edwards* was dispatched to retrieve the blimp, which continued to drift. Later news reports that the C-5 crashed into the Atlantic and was found by a passing British ship turned out to be false. There were even reports that the C-5 may have been sighted over Ireland, but these were never substantiated. The C-5 was never seen again.

On the same day the C-5 broke loose from its moorings, the British government announced plans to send the airship R-34 on a transatlantic flight to Cape May, C-5's home base. That airship successfully crossed the Atlantic, becoming the first aircraft to make the crossing from east to west non-stop.

On the evening of the 16th a large crowd gathered to watch the three American aircraft as they taxied out together and headed down the Bay in formation for take-off. The NC-4 lifted off but the other two did not. They signalled for the *Aroostook*'s small boat to come alongside so that they could remove more weight. The NC-4 had returned and landed. All three

The US Navy C-5 blimp blew away in a gale not long after it had landed. (Library of Congress)

again took up positions as far back in the harbour as possible and at 1800 they started once again. Bouncing across the crests they took to the air, the NC-4 most easily of all.

The route between Trepassey Bay and Ponta Delgada in the Azores was marked by a string of 25 'station' destroyers at approximately 50-mile intervals. The radio direction finders worked poorly but each destroyer was to make smoke, or if at night, swing a searchlight from the surface to straight up into the night sky. Star shells were fired and a report by radio of the passing of the aircraft was made and the next destroyer alerted. Formation was maintained until dark when Towers ordered running lights be turned on. The lights on the NC-4 came on but not on the other two aircraft. Realising this he ordered the formation to open up to reduce the danger of collision.

NC-4 in flight. (Library of Congress)

As they headed south, they expected to run into increasingly better weather and although the weather remained good through the night, with the morning came rain, thick low clouds and fog.

In NC-3, Towers caught a glimpse of a ship through a hole in the clouds. In the fog he mistook it for one of the 'station' destroyers. It was in fact the cruiser *Marblehead* returning from Europe. Based on the sighting, Towers changed course. This was a costly mistake. The NC-3 ran into heavy rain squalls and tried different altitudes all to no avail. The clouds were so thick they could not see their wing tips. Turbulent air shook the wallowing aircraft and with the primitive instruments of the time it was difficult to determine the attitude of the aeroplane. By 11.30 am Towers figured he must be in the vicinity of the islands, but he also knew he was off course. With two hours of fuel remaining and the very real possibility of running into a mountain on one of the islands he decided it would be better to set the aircraft down on the water and wait for the weather to moderate. A descent was made and as they passed through 500 feet they could make out the surface of the ocean. It did not look too bad, so he signalled Commander Richardson, the pilot, to make the landing. Unfortunately they misread the swells, hitting the first one hard before falling into the hollow. They then shot back into the air and smashed into the following wave. Struts on the centre engine buckled, hull frames split, and damage was done to the controls.

Inside the aircraft the shaken crew realised that any further flight could not be resumed. Worse, any attempts at communication were futile. There was little they could do but wait and hope for rescue as the aircraft drifted with the nose down into the wind which, luckily, set it on a course to Ponta Delgada. Two days later the aircraft was in sight of the breakwater.

Towers had the two outboard engines started. Although they vibrated badly, they provided enough power to taxi into the harbour and up to a mooring buoy.

Lieutenant Commander Bellinger in the NC-1 made the same decision as Towers. The aircraft had been flying at an altitude of just 75 feet. Navigation was impossible and down that low they could not reach anyone on the radio. Lieutenant Commander Mitscher was flying the aeroplane and was ordered to land. But when the NC-1 touched down it was buried in a large wave which broke the wing struts and tail beams. The wings began to fill with water, and it was necessary to slash the fabric. The hull had also been damaged and was taking on water which required constant bailing. About three hours after hitting the water they were spotted by the Greek steamer *Ionia* and picked up. A short time later they were transferred to the USS *Gridley*. An attempt was made to take the aircraft in tow, but it was so badly damaged that it was decided to sink it. With two aircraft out, American fortunes now lay with the NC-4.

The NC-4 was also in bad weather and as it continued to deteriorate Read motioned to Stone to take the aircraft up higher. At 3,200 feet the NC-4 broke out of the cloud cover. As they approached the position of the next destroyer, Read gave orders to descend for a visual check. As they entered back into the clouds the aircraft began to buffet and became difficult to fly as had the others. Suddenly a wing dropped, and the aircraft went into a spin. It seems no one realised it until a glimpse of the sun was caught through a break in the clouds. Read shouted for Stone to bring it out of the spin. This he managed to do but it was not an easy task. To bring such a large heavily-loaded aircraft out of a spin in clear weather would have been an accomplishment, but the NC-4 had re-entered solid cloud with zero visibility. With only the rudimentary flight instruments then available, bringing it out of a spin was an amazing feat.

Once Stone had the aircraft under control he again climbed to relative safety above the clouds. Read elected to stay there and use dead reckoning for the islands. In mid-morning the NC-4 passed over an opening in the clouds. Read saw what he thought was a riptide. Examining the two shades of colour below, he realised that the darker mass was land. Read then directed Stone to spiral down to 200 feet. Using time and distance and visual reference they determined they were at the southern tip of Flores, one of the islands that make up the western Azores. Read set a course for Ponta Delgada 250 miles away. A short while later they passed over a 'station' destroyer but it was not long before the weather began to deteriorate again.

NC-4 was the only aircraft to make it to the Azores without serious damage. (Library of Congress)

They were now getting low on fuel and there was certainly not going to be enough to enable them to start searching if they missed Delgada, so Read decided to turn south for Horta on the island of Fayal where the USS *Columbia* was standing by. They landed in the harbour at Horta at 13:23. A tremendous welcome awaited Read and his crew.

Back in St John's there was now a scene of frenzied activity. The Americans' departure had already convinced Hawker that they should make their attempt even if the weather forecasts were less than perfect. But news of their arrival in the Azores sealed matters. It was now or never. Hawker believed his Sopwith had the power advantage over the big, slow flying boats and therefore could still secure national pride as well as the *Daily Mail*'s prize. What they did not know in St John's was that two of the American aircraft were now out of contention and that NC-4 was going to be delayed for several days. It is easy to understand the frustration that he felt after weeks of delays during which he had had the competition to himself only to see other contenders arrive. But his decision to go was to be a costly error of judgement. Having discussed it with Raynham and Morgan, they decided to leave on Sunday.

Early on Sunday, 18 May, the Sopwith *Atlantic* aeroplane was ready to go. Tanks were filled to the brim, flasks of fresh coffee and sandwiches packed, and everything aboard. After saying their farewells and sending respects (and hopes of seeing him at Brooklands) to Raynham who was also getting ready over at Quidi Vidi, it was time to get the Rolls-Royce engine warmed up and ticking over smoothly. Finally, at 3.40 pm local time, Hawker and Grieve climbed aboard and made final preparations for take-off. It was not going to be easy as the aircraft was laden down with fuel and supplies. The wind was about twenty miles an hour east-north-east, and that meant that they had to go diagonally across their L-shaped ground, just touching the hill, and avoiding, if they could, a deepish drainage ditch which ran along the foot of it. All their trial flights both in England and in Newfoundland

Grieve (L) and Hawker (R) lost the advantage they had in being first to arrive in Newfoundland due to a long spell of poor weather but then were forced to start their attempt on receiving news that the NC-4 had left the Azores. (BAE Systems)

had been done with three-quarter loads of petrol, and they knew very well that there would not be too much room with the full load on board. However, all was well. The going was rough, and the hillside made the

Preparing the Sopwith for its Atlantic flight at Mount Pearl. (BAE Systems)

Running up the engine on the Sopwith 'Atlantic'. (BAE Systems)

Harry Hawker taking the Sopwith 'Atlantic' for a test flight from Mount Pearl. (BAE Systems)

aircraft roll a bit, but they missed the ditch by inches and got into the air with a respectable distance to spare between their wheels and the trees. As soon as they were up high enough, Hawker throttled down and began a steady climb out towards the Atlantic and towards the Ireland that he hoped to see inside the next twenty-four hours. As soon as the coast had been passed, he pulled the undercarriage release trigger and away it went into the water. Simultaneously the finger of the air speed indicator went over to another seven miles an hour.

The sky was bright and clear to start with, but they had only climbed a few thousand feet, and they had only been flying for about ten minutes when they saw the persistent Newfoundland fog hanging around the coast. But it was no cause for concern as the fog was never more than a few hundred feet thick, and they knew they would soon be leaving it behind. Grieve had been able to observe the sea long enough to get a fair drift reading, and the fog bank didn't interfere with his navigation as it gave him the sort of horizon he wanted, being quite flat and distinct.

At 1900 a signalman at the maritime lookout on Signal Hill above St John's reported that the Sopwith had passed out of sight in a south-easterly direction at a height of 8,000 feet. That was the last time they were seen.

Back on the ground at Quidi Vidi things were not going so well. As had been agreed, Hawker had discussed their departure with Raynham and so they too had set about preparing for the flight. As the Martinsyde was slightly faster than the Sopwith, Raynham and Morgan were quietly confident that they could take off as much as an hour later and still pass Hawker before they reached the Irish coast. The cross-wind was proving problematic and two attempts to take off had to be aborted.

At 4.40 pm local time, the *Raymor* surged forward, quickly gathering speed. Within a moment its wheels broke from the surface. The race was on! But it had barely covered two hundred yards when a savage crosswind caught the aircraft and flipped it over. Onlookers stared in shock at the violence they had just witnessed, others rushed over to the stricken aircraft fearing the worst. Both crewmen were slightly injured, but a glass splinter had pierced Morgan's skull and so he was sent back to England on doctor's orders.

Raynham meanwhile resolved to repair the aircraft and make another attempt at the earliest opportunity with Lieutenant C.H. Biddlecombe joining him as navigator who was not to arrive in Newfoundland until 14 June.

Alcock and Brown had spent that Sunday travelling to Ferryland to the south of St John's where, it had been reported, they might find a suitable landing ground. Yet again it proved a fruitless journey and it was while they were heading back that they heard the news that Hawker and Grieve had been reported missing. Initial reports raised hopes that they would be found quickly, but hopes were then dashed as it was impossible to confirm the messages. Although it had been made clear that the Atlantic teams were

The ill-fated Martinsyde Raymor ready to begin its take off run. (NARA)

The inability of the heavily loaded Raymor to get airborne resulted in a heavy crash which took weeks to repair and cost Raynham his chance of winning the prize. (NARA)

competing as private individuals and commercial enterprises, such was Hawker's reputation that the Admiralty dispatched several destroyers to begin the search and two RAF squadrons based in Ireland were tasked with helping the search. The news spread quickly all over the world, but nowhere was it more intensely felt than amongst the small group of airmen gathered in the Cochrane Hotel who had shared their hopes and discussed their plans. The atmosphere turned gloomy.

A thousand miles away Hawker and Grieve were oblivious to the drama caused by their disappearance. For them, the flight had been going well and as far as the weather was concerned everything looked quite good for some hours. They were comfortably motoring along at about 10,000 feet with little cloud between themselves and the great expanse of sky above them. The engine was roaring contentedly as though it would run like that until the tanks were bone dry. The air speed indicator was showing a respectable 105 miles an hour. There were practically no bumps and Hawker felt that he could pretty well let the machine fly itself so long as he held her on the course that Grieve had laid down. They could be forgiven for feeling confident and having that tremendous sense of wellbeing that comes from looking out over the expanse of sky at altitude as the sun begins to drop below the horizon.

By about 10 pm all the blue in the sky had turned to purple. The warm glint of the sun had faded from the polished edges of the struts, and the clouds below had become dull, patchy and grey. Occasionally they got a glimpse of the ocean beneath them. But a quarter of an hour later the weather conditions had noticeably changed for the worse. The sky became hazy and thick so that they could not see anything below them clearly, although they could see well enough that there was some pretty heavy stuff ahead. There was only one thing to do: as it wasn't very solid, they just poked the aircraft's nose into it and pushed through. But it was very bumpy, and now and then they were splashed by a slant of rain. However, that didn't matter as they were quite warm and comfortable and were expecting soon to leave the little patch of nasty weather behind them.

They had been flying for about another hour when Hawker glanced at the water circulation thermometer and saw that it was a good bit higher than it ought to have been, although they were still slightly climbing. Clearly not all was well with the water, as the temperature did not go down as he expected it to when he opened the shutters over the radiator a little. As they carried on, they didn't seem to be able to get clear of the clouds which now began to appear thicker and heavier than ever. There was also enough of them at lower levels to prevent any chance of getting any glimpse of the sea.

By this time they had altered course a little to northward, as from the information they had received from the meteorological station, they were expecting that the wind would tend to go more into that quarter. But it was proving none too easy to hold the course. The cloud formations they were running into were formidable and giving them a bumpy ride. Climbing higher would have meant eating into their fuel which, of course, they needed to preserve as efficiently as possible. Another reason why they didn't want to climb was the increasing temperature of the water. In the end they just had to go around the clouds as best they could, but there were so many of them that Grieve never had a chance to take a sight on the stars.

A little later, the moon rose and brightened things up and lifted their spirits. The water temperature in the radiator had risen from 168 to 176 degrees Fahrenheit, in spite of the shutters being wide open, and it was obvious that something serious was wrong with the cooling system. Apart from the water temperature, the Rolls-Royce engine was running absolutely perfectly, as was the rest of the aeroplane, and despite the weather Hawker and Grieve were happy and warm enough.

At about 11:30 Hawker decided that something had to be done to keep the water temperature down. He had already reached the conclusion that the most probable cause was a collection of rust and debris that had shaken loose in the radiator and was blocking the filter which was there to prevent any solid substances from getting into the pump.

As an experienced and skilled pilot, Hawker knew that sometimes it was possible to clear this sort of blockage by stopping the engine and nose-diving. This gave the accumulation a chance to spread itself and the filter to clear, leaving the rust and dirt at the bottom edge instead of all over it. At that point there were few other options, so down went her nose. Quietly they dropped from 12,000 to about 9,000 feet. Hawker then started the engine up again and was tremendously relieved to see that the temperature remained at a moderate level even though they were soon climbing again. However, this was only a temporary solution and if they had to do the clearing process often it would mean that they would waste a lot of petrol. This they could not afford to do as the wind was now increasingly against them.

An hour later, at 12.30 pm, the thermometer was back up to 175 degrees. They were now about 800 miles out over the ocean and the weather was showing no signs of improving. They were being forced into continuing their cloud-dodging tactics, burning up precious fuel as they did so. Again Hawker put the aircraft into a dive, but this time they were out of luck. It did not clear the filter, and when they started to climb up the temperature rose perilously close to boiling point. So he tried again, but things only got worse and soon the water started boiling in earnest.

They had nineteen gallons in the engine, but she was pulling about 200 horse power and once she started boiling, in spite of the intense cold it would not take long for the water to evaporate. After a second attempt to clear the blockage failed, Hawker took the machine up to 12,000 feet and reduced throttle, so that the aeroplane was barely moving. At that altitude he hoped to give the water every chance to cool even if it only produced a small drop in temperature. The top wing was covered with ice from the radiator, and steam was spouting out like a little geyser from a tiny hole in the middle of it. But the tactic seemed to work for a while as they were able to keep the temperature just a little below the fateful 212 degrees.

They were now finding it a lot easier to keep on course, for the moon was well up, and at 12,000 feet they were above most of the clouds. It meant that Grieve was able to take an observation on the stars which occasionally peeped out through gaps, mostly to the north. But at about 6 o'clock in the morning they found themselves confronted with a bank of black clouds as solid as a range of mountains and rearing up in fantastic and menacing formations. They were at least 15,000 feet high, so it was obviously useless to try and get over the whole lot. But when they couldn't fly round them, they found going through them was out of the question after they had had one try at it. They also tried going over some of the lower ones, but each time they rose the water temperature rose too, boiling the water. So they had to abandon that strategy. Apart from the overheating, Hawker had had no other trouble at all in flying the aircraft; with the aid of the few stars they saw occasionally it was quite easy to set the trim, and when they got engulfed in the blackness of the clouds every now and then they were able to keep it straight and level with the compass and the bubble.

But they could not go on like this for the rest of the journey. Very reluctantly they realised that as they couldn't go up, they would have to come down. They descended to about 6,000 feet but found the sky blacker than ever. Descending another 1,000 feet they found things a good deal brighter with the sun just beginning to rise up over the horizon and help them on their way. Grieve's observations on the stars had shown that they were now on course and well in the 'Steamer Lane', the route followed by many of the ships that crisscrossed the Atlantic.

The water boiling was not helping matters. They realised just how much water had been lost when they dropped down to 1,000 ft and when Hawker went to open the throttle and restart the engine, it failed to fire up. The problem was that so much water had boiled off that there was not enough in the jackets to gradually cool the engine, which meant that the engine went stone cold very quickly even though steam was coming out of the radiator relief pipe for a considerable time.

Hawker shouted to Grieve to get busy on the petrol pump. This he was able to do except that he pumped so hard that he managed to push the carburettor needle valves right off their seats which flooded the jets with petrol. Nothing happened at all except that the ocean was rising up to meet them at an alarming rate. They were gliding downwind at a pretty good speed and they could now see that the ocean below was rough. Hawker realised this could be a very hard landing and that if he remained where he was Grieve would probably get badly injured as he would be shot forward head first onto the petrol tank. Hawker smacked him on the back and yelled to him that he was going to land.

By now they were about ten feet above the very uninviting-looking waves. Then, just as they braced themselves for the impact, they had the biggest stroke of luck. Thanks to Grieve's pumping, the engine at last fired. Hawker gave the motor a good mouthful of throttle and it roared away as if there had not been a problem. The dive flattened and then turned into a climb. Soon they were back up to a healthy altitude and very relieved to be there.

Had they hit the water they would not have stood a chance. With the wind pushing them along they were going too fast for this to be anything but a very violent crash. Almost certainly they would have been injured. The aeroplane would have been badly damaged, and more than likely, they would have been unable to launch the boat even if they weren't badly injured and incapacitated. It had been a close shave.

This narrowest of escapes made them realise that they probably were not going to reach the Irish coast. Although they still had plenty of fuel, the lack of water was the problem and what they had left might keep them flying for another hour or two but that would still not be enough. They now decided to fly around in search of a ship. To do this they steered a sort of zig-zag course, dodging the clouds and squalls of rain, as well as keeping down low owing to the clouds. If they couldn't spot one, then they would simply have to make the best landing they could, launch the boat, set off their big Holmes flare which would last for an hour at least, and hope for the best. They also had plenty of Very lights to fall back on, and if it looked like it might be a long wait for rescue, they had plenty of food, for they had scarcely touched any on the flight beyond drinking a fair amount of coffee and munching chocolate. Indeed neither of them had felt like eating at all.

They flew around for two hours or so in weather that was getting worse rather than better. There were rain squalls and the wind was getting stronger, gustier and bumpier every minute. The sea was also getting rougher. At least they did not have the weight of the undercarriage, but the waves were getting high enough that even a seaplane would have struggled to stay upright.

They were in a frightening predicament as although they knew they were landing on the steamer route, there was enough fog around to hide them from view even if a ship was quite close.

Suddenly a hull loomed out of the fog and they knew that their luck had changed. Hawker shouted with joy and even the otherwise reserved Grieve felt like joining in.

The ship they saw was the *Mary*, a Danish merchantman, and she was sailing towards England. They flew around her, fired three Very light distress signals, and kept close by until her crew began to appear on the decks. Then they flew off a couple of miles or so along her course.

Using the cresting waves to give him an idea of how strong the wind was, Hawker came round into wind. It was a high sea and he did his best to put the aircraft down as gently as possible. The aircraft settled quite nicely and, thanks to her partly empty tanks, rode clear of the water, although now and then the waves sloshed right over them and soon started smashing the wings.

They had no difficulty in detaching their little boat and getting it launched, even though the aircraft was sinking fast, although they did not expect it to go down altogether.

Their life-saving suits worked well and kept them reasonably dry. Soon the *Mary* was near them and hurried to get a lifeboat out. It was hard work in the rough sea. Even though she was only two hundred yards away it was an hour and a half before she could get to Hawker and Grieve and take them off. They had run a line out to the boat from the ship and were soon hauled in. Because of the heavy sea it was impossible for them to salvage anything off the aircraft, but a good part of the machine and the mail bag was picked up days later by the *Lake Charlotteville* and brought into Falmouth. The time was 8.30 pm, fourteen and a half hours after they had left Newfoundland.

As the wireless had not worked in the aircraft due to the engine magnetos disrupting reception, no one was aware of Hawker and Grieve's fate. Once on board the ship, they had hoped they would be able to use the ship's wireless to let the waiting world know that they were safe. But this was not to be as the ship did not have a wireless. What's more, the storm got steadily worse, forcing the ship's captain to heave to. For the next few days they made very little headway and what progress they did make took them further northwards away from the shipping lanes. In the absence of any news, the world assumed the worst. It is a measure of the respect and esteem that Hawker was held in that the story was picked up by newspapers all over the world. The King even sent a message of condolence to Hawker's wife Muriel even though she was adamant that he was still alive. In addition, the *Daily Mail* offered £5,000 each to Hawker's and Grieve's next of kin.

News of Hawker's and Grieve's disappearance had cast a sombre mood over the remaining aviators in Newfoundland as thick and grey as the weather. It reminded them of just how risky this crossing was.

Raynham had already made arrangements to repair his Martinsyde for another attempt. He also invited Alcock and Brown to use his ground for erecting the Vimy when it arrived. A similar invitation was given by Captain Fenn, who Hawker had left in charge of the Sopwith party.

Although neither airfield would be suitable for the Vimy's final take-off, they accepted Raynham's very sporting offer and arranged to build up the Vimy, which was expected to arrive any day, on his airfield at Quidi Vidi, while continuing the search for a more suitable field.

By 25 May, the *Mary* had arrived off the Butt of Lewis. Using flags they signalled the Lloyds station that Hawker and Grieve were on board. From there they were transferred to a naval ship, the destroyer *Woolston*, which took them to Scapa Flow where they received a wonderful welcome

The wreckage of the Sopwith was eventually retrieved and brought back to London. (BAE Systems)

from the Grand Fleet and Admiral Freemantle. From there Hawker sent a message to the *Daily Mail*:

> HMS Revenge, Scapa, May 25 via Aberdeen, 10.35pm. My machine stopped owing to the water filter in the feed-pipe from the radiator to the water cock being blocked up with refuse, such as solder and the like shaking loose in the radiator.
>
> It was no fault of the motor (Rolls-Royce). The motor ran absolutely perfectly from start to finish even when all the water had boiled away. I had no trouble landing in the sea. We were picked up by the tramp ship 'Mary' after being in the water for one and a half hours.

The congratulatory telegrams began to pour in including one from the King to Hawker's wife, Muriel:

> The King rejoices with you and the nation on the happy rescue of your gallant husband. His Majesty trusts that he may long be spared to you.

When they arrived at London's King's Cross station a crowd of over 100,000 people were waiting to greet them. There were so many people that it was difficult to open the carriage door and it was only when some Australian soldiers intervened and carried them shoulder high that they were able to get to their waiting car. Ropes had been tied to the car so that the soldiers could pull it but with so many people crowding in little progress could be made. Hawker then climbed up onto the horse of a mounted policeman. The policeman graciously gave up his horse to Hawker so that he could lead the procession to the Royal Aero Club's headquarters in Clifford Street where an enthusiastic reception awaited them.

The next day King George V announced that he would personally present both men with the Air Force Cross for gallantry in the air – the first ever personal investitures. Afterwards at a lunch at the Savoy hosted by the *Daily Mail*, Hawker, as the first pilot to fly over 1,000 miles of water without touching down, was awarded a consolation prize of five thousand pounds.

Now, with the news that Hawker and Grieve were safe, the mood lifted. Alcock and Brown got a further boost to their morale when on 26 May the Vickers mechanics arrived with the crates containing their aeroplane and engines. The crates had to be hauled up onto carts and transported to their

Grieve, Muriel Hawker, Harry Hawker. (BAE Systems)

Although they failed in their attempt Hawker and Grieve were greeted as heroes on their return.

hastily prepared airfield at Quidi Vidi. With Sopwith and Martinsyde both out of contention, it looked as if the race was now between Handley Page and Vickers with Handley Page the clear favourites. They had the best airfield, best accommodation, fuel, the biggest aircraft built by the Allies powered by four of the mighty Rolls-Royce Eagles. They had already flown the aircraft, but it seemed to have some problems. In what might be considered typical of the naval approach, Admiral Kerr seemed determined not to attempt the flight until his plane was in perfect condition. His prevaricating gave Alcock and Brown a chance to catch up.

Above: Vimy assembly at Quidi Vidi. (BAE Systems)

Right: (BAE Systems)

John Alcock (in cockpit) kept a watchful eye on progress. (BAE Systems)

Alcock (in cockpit), kept a close interest as the Vimy was re-assembled. (BAE Systems)

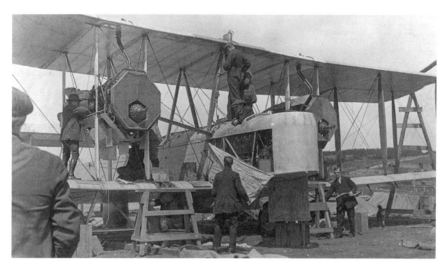

The Vickers team threw themselves into the task of rebuilding the Vimy out in the open. (BAE Systems)

The Vimy had to be fenced off from curious on-lookers as the aircraft came together. (BAE Systems)

The Vickers mechanics set to work at once reassembling the machine. All the work was carried out in the open air, days of welding, soldering, sanding and stitching. Building an aircraft of this size and this quickly would have been hard enough back in the factory but doing it in an open field with the elements conspiring to make the task so much harder presented the team with many obstacles and required much improvisation. For example, sheer legs had to be constructed out of scaffolding poles. Raynham generously let them use his hangar as a store.

All the Vickers party worked hard and cheerfully from early dawn until dark, each man putting in strenuous shifts from twelve to fourteen hours a day. Two mechanics remained on guard each night, while the remainder drove about three miles to their billets.

Vickers engineers had to manhandle the partially re-built Vimy to a different part of the field at Quidi Vidi. (BAE Systems)

Re-building the Vimy in poor weather out in the open made the task even harder. (BAE Systems)

On Tuesday, 27 May, the crew of the NC-4 was up before dawn. The engines and radio were checked out and on the signal from Read, Elmer Stone advanced the throttles and the big flying boat lifted off in the early morning light bound for Lisbon. As they had done for the journey from Newfoundland, a chain of destroyers extended between the Azores and Lisbon. The weather was good and as the NC-4 passed over each destroyer the ship radioed a message of her passage to the base ship *Melville* at Ponta Delgada and the cruiser *Rochester* in Lisbon who in turn reported to the Navy Department in Washington. At 19.30 the flashing light from the Coba da Roca lighthouse was spotted and the NC-4 passed over the coastline. The big aircraft turned southward towards the Tagus estuary and Lisbon. At 20:01 on 27 May 1919, after flying for nine hours and forty-three minutes, the NC-4's keel sliced into the waters of the Tagus. The welcome was tumultuous. A transatlantic flight, the first one in the history of the world, was an accomplished fact.

Early in the morning of 30 May the NC-4 departed Lisbon for Plymouth, England. But an overheating engine forced the NC-4 to set down in the Mondego River. The radiator had developed a leak and was repaired but

Flight crew of the successful NC-4: From left to right: Chief Mechanic E.C. Rhodes, USN; Lt. J.L. Breese, USNRF; Lt.(jg) W. Hinton,USN; Lt. E.F. Stone, USCG; Lt.Cmdr. A.S. Read, USN.

because of a low tide condition it became too late in the day to take off and reach Plymouth before dark so Read proceeded to Ferrol in northern Spain to spend the night. They were back in the air the next morning and as they approached Plymouth a formation of Royal Air Force seaplanes escorted the NC-4 into the harbour. A British warship fired a twenty-one gun salute as the NC-4 circled. The Lord Mayor of Plymouth received Commander Read and his crew and from Plymouth they went to London where they were decorated by King George V. President Woodrow Wilson, who was at the Peace Conference in Paris, sent for them, congratulated them for their outstanding achievement, and introduced them to all present.

Of course national pride dictated that Alcock and Brown had wanted to be the first across the Atlantic, as had Hawker and Grieve, but they were not going to be distracted from the task in hand, that is, they would be the first to fly non-stop across the ocean in less than seventy-two hours. But at times it seemed that the Vimy might never get airborne as the Vickers team encountered a thousand and one difficulties. Even people not directly involved came to lend a hand where they could. The reporters representing the *Daily Mail*, the *New York Times* and the *New York World* were often called on to help when extra manpower was required. One of the reporters, a Mr Klauber, gave Alcock and Brown his electric torch when theirs failed at the last moment.

It was a nerve-jangling time as the machine approached completion. Each day produced some new difficulty. The time Alcock had spent

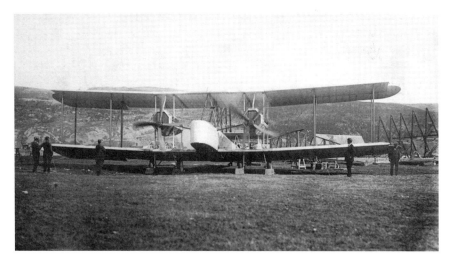

Vimy with engines running. Alcock's meticulous oversight of the Vimy's re-assembly including filtering the water and fuel gave them the best chance of success. (BAE Systems)

overseeing the Vimy's assembly back at Brooklands paid dividends as he kept his head and his temper firmly in check while supervising his mechanics' work.

As the parts of the Vimy were put together and it began to look like a complete aeroplane, it attracted more and more visitors. It seemed amazing that so many spectators, who seemed to have no other occupation, spent hours in leaning on the nearest fence and watching them work. Eventually there were so many it became necessary to build a temporary enclosure around the machine. But even that did not keep the curious at a distance. Those that simply came to watch were not a problem but there were also those who could not keep their hands to themselves even if it meant damaging the aircraft. The testing of the fabric's firmness with the point of an umbrella was a favourite pastime, and more than once they had to disperse small parties who were found leaning against the trailing-edges. One man even held his lighted cigar against a wing and was quite annoyed when asked to keep at a distance.

But they were still no nearer to finding a suitable site for a strip of land from which they could take off in their heavily laden Vimy. Every day seemed to bring fresh hope and optimism that this increasingly urgent problem would be resolved only for it to end in yet another disappointment. For example, one day a telegram arrived from a landowner in Harbour Grace offering what he called an ideal field. Alcock raced off to inspect

On days when weather permitted, crowds would flock to Quidi Vidi to watch the Vickers team at work. (BAE Systems)

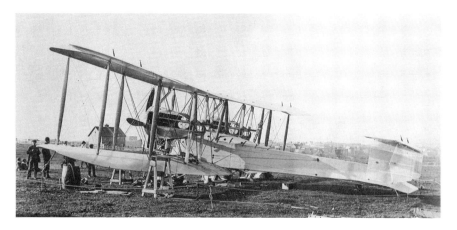

The Vimy was almost complete by the first week of June. (BAE Systems)

On-lookers were never short of advice for the Vickers team as they re-built the Vimy. (BAE Systems)

and secure it; but when he returned in the evening his one-sided grin told Brown that they were still out of luck: 'The ideal airfield' was a meadow about 150 by 300 yards—and the price demanded for its hire was $25,000 plus the cost of getting it ready and an indemnity for all damage. The going rate for buying land in Newfoundland at that time was about thirty-five cents an acre.

Alcock (L) and Brown (R) in conversation with Eric Platford of Rolls-Royce (C). (BAE Systems)

Then, as if by chance, a local farmer, Charles Lester, who had organised all the carting of crates to Quidi Vidi, offered them a field about three miles away at a more reasonable cost, at a place called Monday's Pool. It turned out to be a large meadow, half on a hill and with a swamp at the bottom. It possessed, nevertheless, a level surface of about three hundred yards, running east-west.

They examined the site, and although it was just about alright, Alcock and Brown felt they needed more space for the take-off. They paced out four other fields on the hilltop and found that by including them they could obtain a full run of 500 yards. The owners of this additional ground wanted extortionate prices for its use, but after much haggling they struck a deal with them.

Thirty labourers, with pick and shovel, set to work to prepare the airfield by removing hillocks, blasting boulders and levelling walls and fences. The expense was enormous – over $1,300 – but the work was completed, and well within time for the trial flight.

While Alcock had been busy looking for a suitable landing ground and supervising the unpacking and assembly of the Vimy, Brown set to work on setting up his navigation equipment. He rigged up a receiving station on the roof of the Cochrane Hotel, and with the consent and help of Lieutenant Clare of the Mount Pearl Naval Wireless Station, he practised the sending and receiving of wireless messages and tuning in on various wave-lengths.

However, the weather was still playing havoc with the Vickers engineers trying to assemble the aircraft. For three days, driving wind and rain blew through Newfoundland. As the Vimy was being assembled in the open there was little they could do but cover the engines and airframe with tarpaulins. Once better conditions arrived the whole team made a big effort to get the aircraft built. Soon the body of the Vimy started to take shape, growing slowly into some semblance of a complete aeroplane. Once the wings were in place, the Rolls-Royce engineer was able to get started, checking every little detail of the motors, so that there should be no avoidable trouble on that account. In a move that may have contributed significantly to their chances of success, Alcock had noticed that the local water was heavy in minerals and sediment. To counter this, Alcock asked for the water for the radiator to be filtered several times and then boiled in a steel barrel. The process got rid of any impurities that could clog the engine's cooling system, something that Hawker lived to regret and delayed the Handley Page attempt enough to enable Alcock and Brown to overtake them.

The spectators from St John's who arrived daily to watch proceedings showed much interest in the boiling process and asked many questions. They seemed content with the explanation that the mechanics were boiling the gasoline so as to remove all water. It seems amazing that no one from Handley Page felt compelled to quiz Alcock and Brown on this as they were experiencing problems with their radiators. Several onlookers even asked whether they filled the planes with gas to make them lighter. Others were disappointed because they did not intend to drop their undercarriage over the sea, as Hawker had done, and prophesied that such neglect would lead to failure.

With no time or space to build a wooden Hangar, the Vickers engineers had to improvise as best they could in the difficult weather conditions. (BAE Systems)

The fuel was filtered through a very fine copper mesh to make sure there were no impurities. The first batch had turned into a gel-like goo and it was good fortune that when Vickers' manager Max Mueller arrived in Newfoundland just before the flight that he brought a new consignment of fuel with him. (BAE Systems)

The morning of Monday, 9 June, dawned clear and dry. The Vimy was ready, assembled in just thirteen days from the first crate being opened. Meanwhile, over at Harbour Grace, Admiral Kerr had requested yet another radiator change as he felt they were 'not quite up to snuff'. It would be days before replacements arrived from England and although Raynham's repairs were progressing well, he too was still not ready to fly. There was also news that the R-34 airship was ready to make its attempt from East Fortune on Scotland's Firth of Forth. The odds of a successful flight now swung in favour of Alcock and Brown.

The conditions were perfect for them to take the Vimy up for its first flight and so they decided to take off that afternoon. They hoped to keep the trial flight as secret as possible, but word got out and the crowds began to head out to Quidi Vidi even before they had warmed and tested the engines.

The weather continued to hold as they taxied out and took off. Everything seemed to be running smoothly. Indeed Brown described the Vimy as being as 'nippy as a single seater scout'. They headed directly westward, passing over the sea for some fifteen minutes. It was a clear day, and the sea reflected the sky's vivid blue. Near the coast it was streaked and spotted by the glistening white of icebergs and the evanescent appearances and disappearances of white-caps.

With the machine and engines all working perfectly, the conditions were also perfect for Brown to test his navigational instruments. Although they worked well, the wireless could not be made to work at all.

Alcock then turned the Vimy and brought them back over St John's at a height of 4,000 feet. Newfoundland from above looked even more bleak and rugged than it did from the ground; and they could see that landing grounds were simply not possible on the eastern side of it.

They had already decided to land the Vimy at their newly-prepared site at Lester's Field. A smoky 'smudge' fire had been lit to help them pick out the spot. Alcock made a perfect landing, running uphill. However, there was now a moment of drama as a fence at the end of the field rushed up to meet them. If the aircraft could not be slowed down their successful first flight was going to end in an accident. The Vimy ran on and topped the brow, but Alcock, using all his considerable skill and experience, avoided a collision by opening up the starboard engine. The surge of power was enough to swing the aircraft round before she came to a standstill. The flight had barely lasted fifteen minutes but it was an undoubted success, much to Alcock and Brown's relief.

Once they had dismounted, they pushed the machine down the hill to the most sheltered part of the field. The hangar they planned to put the Vimy in was still unfinished and so it would have to remain in the open. There was little they could do but tie it down with pegs and ropes and hope for the best. They also took the precaution of roping off a space around the aircraft to keep the more persistent spectators at a safe distance.

Brown dismounted the wireless generator for examination, and the next day took it to Mount Pearl Wireless Station, where Lieutenant Clare helped him to locate the fault and repair it.

But a far more serious worry now confronted them. The fuel they had intended to carry was a mixture of gasoline and benzol, sent from England. On examination they found it had changed into a peculiar kind of gel. It was sticky and had the consistency of India rubber wetted with gasoline; but when dry it reduced to a powder. Naturally they could not afford the risk of letting such a deposit clog the engines' filters and perhaps cause engine failure – a transatlantic flyer's worst nightmare.

It was not definitely proved that the precipitate resulted from the mixture of gasoline and benzol, but so much depended on having good quality fuel

The Vimy had to be tethered down to protect it In the high winds. (BAE Systems)

that they dared not use any that was doubtful. The problem was how to find enough fuel of the quality required. Raynham, as much a sportsman as ever, offered his spare stock. Their problem was resolved when a new shipment arrived, brought over by Vickers' works manager Maxwell Muller.

Muller was responsible for committing Vickers to the Atlantic challenge and had been the man who hired both Alcock and Brown. He was a dynamic personality who was adept at getting people to believe that anything was possible. On a more mundane level, he was also responsible for paying the mounting pile of bills that had built up over the previous month.

Once again, the weather closed in. A near gale blew through the Vickers team's hastily improvised site at the newly-named Lester's Field. There had been no time to build a hangar and so the Vimy was out in the open, tethered down with ropes and covered in tarpaulins as well as possible. A round-the-clock watch was maintained in case she broke free. Ears strained for the sound of ripping fabric as the winds blew.

On Thursday the 12th the wind dropped enough to enable Alcock to make a second flight to test out the wireless and one or two minor corrections he had made since the first flight. Once again everything except the wireless was satisfactory. The transmitter worked well for a short time, but afterwards the insulation on a small transformer in the transmitter failed, giving Brown a violent shock. After a short time in the air, Alcock made another satisfactory landing. He felt that they were now ready to make their attempt on the Atlantic. The only problem now was that the weather was still less than stable.

Lieutenant Clements, the RAF meteorological officer, was doing his best to create forecasts from transmissions from ships out at sea, but these were intermittent and not necessarily as up to date as the waiting airmen needed. Besides his own work he had now undertaken the duties of Major Partridge, official starter for the Royal Aero Club back in London. Each departing aircraft taking part in the competition had to carry the Royal Aero Club's seal to prove that the aircraft were not switched between Newfoundland and Ireland. This he did without any superfluous ceremony. Alcock and Brown hoped they could leave on Friday the 13th, Alcock's lucky number.

But Friday the 13th was not to be his lucky day. The day dawned with the noise of the rain driving against the windows in the Cochrane Hotel. White crests whipped up by the wind coming off the Atlantic topped the waves down in the harbour. In the hotel kitchen, Agnes Dooley began her daily routine of preparing sandwiches and brewing a flask of coffee just in case today should be 'the day'. Many weeks had passed since she began this morning ritual, first for Hawker, then Raynham and now Alcock and Brown. Clements' forecasts did not seem to offer much hope that today would be any different. But Alcock and Brown headed up to the airfield all the same.

By the time they arrived the rain had at least stopped even if strong gusts still whipped through. The ever-optimistic Alcock pushed Clements for as much information has he could get and although he reckoned the storm would last the rest of the day and possibly into the next, he could not be one hundred per cent certain given the patchy nature of the data he was getting. For Alcock, acutely aware that the Handley Page would soon be ready, the frustration of the delay was too much. If there was a chance, even the slimmest of chances that they could get away, then they were going to take it. He ordered the aircraft be prepared for flight. Everyone who was there lent a hand in rolling the heavy drums of petrol and oil across the soft ground. Fuelling the aircraft was a slow process as the fuel had to be pumped up by hand through special filters. Alcock as ever was on hand, watching eagle-eyed over the process to make sure not even the slightest piece of debris made it into the tanks. Fully loaded, the Vimy held 870 gallons of petrol and forty gallons of oil stored in the normal tanks as well has in the newly added ones in the bomb bay. As the aircraft had never been fully loaded before, everyone looked on anxiously as the Vimy began to take the weight. The concern was that if she sank too deeply into the turf, she would be unable to move. Suddenly one of the mechanics yelled out, pointing to the underside of the aircraft. The damage was obvious, a shock absorber mounted on the axle had sheered in two. There was nothing to be done but to unload the aircraft and repair the broken part. It was the start of a long night for the Vickers mechanics.

The work took the Vickers engineers most of the night but as the first grey light of dawn began to brighten the sky, the wind began to drop. According to Brown a large black cat, its tail held high in a comical curve, sauntered by the transatlantic machine as they stood by it; and such a cheerful omen made them more than ever anxious to start. They would need as much luck as they could get.

Two other black cats, their mascots, were already stowed away in the little cupboard in the tail section of the Vimy: Lucky Jim and Twinkletoe were woolen toy cats destined to be the first air passengers across the Atlantic. Lucky Jim had an enormous head, an untidy ribbon and a hopeful expression; Twinkletoe was daintily diminutive and, from the tip of her upright tail to the tip of her stuffed nose, expressed surprise and anxiety. Friends had given them other good luck tokens such as bunches of white heather.

'Strong westerly wind. Conditions otherwise fairly favourable' was the brief forecast from the meteorological officer given at 4 am. Alcock and Brown had already decided to leave on the fourteenth, given even half a chance. They wanted to avoid at all costs being worn down by false hopes and endless disappointments while waiting for ideal conditions.

At early dawn they were at Lester's Field, searching the sky for clues and pressing Lieutenant Clements, the Royal Air Force weather expert, for any information on what the weather was doing further out over the Atlantic. His reports were favourable; but a hefty wind was blowing across the airfield from the west in uneven gusts, and everybody was of the view that there was little to lose if take-off was postponed for a few hours, in the expectation that the wind would die down.

As the sun rose in the sky, Alcock ran the engines and found them to be in perfect condition. Everything was checked one last time. No faults were found with the grey-winged machine, inert but fully loaded, and complete to the last split-pin.

Inside the cockpit, Brown was to sit on the port side and Alcock on the right. Between them lay a large battery for heating their bulky flying suits. A sextant was clipped to the dashboard in front of Brown's position. The

Vimy at Lester's Field. (BAE Systems)

Vimy prepared for flight at Lester's Field. (BAE Systems)

course and distance calculators were fastened to the fuselage at his side. Underneath him was a glass plate, the drift indicator, which would enable him to make calculations by observing the motion of waves. The Baker navigating machine, charts and the log lay on the floor. By twisting round in his seat, Brown could reach the small locker behind him which held a Very pistol and an electric torch. The torch was for inspecting the gauges at night and the Very pistol for signalling if they were forced down into the sea.

95

Brown helped into the cockpit. (BAE Systems)

Drums of fuel lined up for the lengthy process of filling the Vimy's tanks. (BAE Systems)

Although the bomb racks had been replaced with tanks for extra fuel, one of these, shaped like a boat, could be used as a life-saving raft if they had to put down into the sea. This tank was positioned so that it would be the first to be emptied of gasoline. The fittings allowed its detachment, ready for floating, while the machine lost height in a glide.

Alcock and Brown wrestle into their bulky flying suits specially made for them by Burberry. (BAE Systems)

The tanks had been filled to the brim during the night, so all that remained for them to do was load their personal luggage, which consisted only of toilet kit and food: sandwiches, Caley's chocolate, Horlicks Malted Milk, and two thermos flasks of coffee. A small cupboard fitted into the tail contained emergency rations. These were for use in case of disaster, as the tail of the aeroplane would remain clear of the waves for a long while after the nose had submerged.

A mail bag had been taken on board a day earlier. It contained 197 letters, for each of which the postal officials at St John's had provided a special stamp. Even back then these stamps became highly collectable: $875 was offered and refused on the Manchester Exchange within two days of one letter's delivery. At a time before telephones and a reliable telegraph network, delivering mail by air was a great leap forward in shortening the time it took to communicate over great distances.

With little left to do, Alcock and Brown settled down in the long grass, ate their last meal in North America and waited for the wind to weaken. As the morning wore on it became clear that the wind was not going to weaken; it remained at about the same strength of 30 mph. But they were done with waiting and they made up their minds to leave at midday.

John Alcock taking a thermos on board. (BAE Systems)

John Alcock in his flying gear. (BAE Systems)

Alcock hands a bag of mail up to Brown. (BAE Systems)

Alcock and Brown's last meal on Newfoundland soil. (BAE Systems)

Having made that decision, Alcock now had to decide in which direction he was going to take off. This was far from straightforward, but to get it wrong would mean that the flight would be over before it even began. They had planned to take off in an easterly direction, although as the wind was coming from the west this would mean taking off with the wind behind them. This was far from ideal for a heavily laden aircraft. However, at least the machine would be facing downhill, and owing to the shape of the airfield, they would have a longer run than if they taxied towards the west. The Vimy was therefore placed in position to suit these arrangements.

But they soon found that the wind really was too strong for such a plan, and that taking off into the wind was going to be less risky. Once again, the mechanics and anyone else willing to lend a hand, dragged the machine to the far end of the airfield, so that it could be prepared for a westerly run.

As the men pushed and pulled the heavy aircraft to the other end of the airfield a sudden gust carried a drag-rope around the undercarriage, tightened one of the wheels against a petrol supply pipe, crushing it. Replacing it took another hour.

They had high hopes that the high winds would drop during the early afternoon, so they sat under the wing-tips at two o'clock and had some lunch, hoping that their next meal would be eaten in Ireland.

But still the wind blew and showed no signs of easing. During the early afternoon, Alcock and Brown agreed to take the conditions as they were and lose no more precious time. At about four o'clock they wriggled into their bulky flying kit. They wore electrically heated clothing and their overalls were made by Burberry's of London. Apart from the mechanics and some reporters, few people were present, for the strong wind had persuaded the day-to-day sightseers from St John's that the start would probably be postponed. When all was ready, they shook hands with Lieutenant Clements, Maxwell Muller and other friends accepting their best wishes for success, posed for some final photographs, climbed onto the machine to scattered applause, and squeezed themselves in the cockpit.

Now all attention was on making a good take-off. While Alcock went through his engine start routine, Brown made certain that his navigation instruments were still in place. The meteorological officer passed him a chart showing the approximate strength and direction of the Atlantic air currents. It indicated that the high westerly wind would drop before they were a hundred miles out to sea, and that the wind velocities for the rest of the journey would not exceed twenty knots, with clear weather over the greater part of the ocean. This was almost too good to be true and sent hopes of a successful soaring flight. But later, when they were over mid-Atlantic, the hopes dissolved in disappointment when the promised clear weather never happened.

The Vimy ready for its historic flight. Note the front skid had been removed. (BAE Systems)

As Alcock shouted 'Contact!' the signal exchanged between pilot and mechanics seemed to have a special momentary significance to Brown sitting next to him, even though he had heard it many times before.

First one and then the other Rolls-Royce Eagle came to life, coughing at first before swelling into a roar as Alcock ran them up before they softened into a subdued murmur when he throttled back. As they warmed up, the aroma of warming oil filled the air. Finally, everything being satisfactory, he disconnected the starting magneto and engine switches to avoid a possible short-circuit which would cut the engines out. Gently he brought the revs up. The Vimy was straining to be let loose but was being held by the mechanics. The two Eagles roared their insistence that they be released so that they could take flight. When it seemed the noise could go no louder, Alcock gave the signal. Chocks were pulled through the eddying grass and the mechanics let their charge go. The Vimy lurched forward, hesitant at first before accelerating eagerly into the westerly wind.

The take-off, up a slight gradient, was difficult. Gusts up to forty-five knots were registered, and there was insufficient room to begin the run dead into the wind. Their particular fear was that a sudden cross-wind might lift the aircraft on one side and cause the machine to heel over. Another danger was the rough surface of the airfield.

But now was not the right moment for doubt. Alcock had everything under control. As the Vimy was carrying a full load, he kept her lumbering along on the ground for as long as he could. After 300 yards it seemed to Brown that they must surely run out of airfield. Then a sudden gust of cross-wind caught them, lifting the left wing. As Alcock fought to keep control, his features fixed in concentration, Brown held his breath; he was a helpless passenger with no role to play in the crazy drama that was unfolding. At four hundred yards, the Vimy began to break contact with the ground, barely perceptible at first. Slowly, painfully slowly, she began to rise, but those pine trees at the end of the field were rushing up to meet them. Brown could feel himself willing the Vimy to lift just a little bit more. He could hardly bring himself to look but then gasped as the trees skimmed beneath them. One of the greatest flights in the history of aviation had begun.

But they were not out of danger yet. The climb out was slow and laboured. A line of hills straight ahead was responsible for much bumpiness in the atmosphere and made climbing difficult. At times the strong wind dropped almost to zero, then rose in eddying blasts. Once or twice their wheels nearly touched the ground again. For those watching from the ground

The start of Alcock and Brown's historic flight. (BAE Systems)

The heavily loaded Vimy struggled to get airborne. (BAE Systems)

it seemed at one point as if the Vimy might have crashed as it disappeared from view behind a hill, before rising up again to their huge relief.

Certainly Alcock's skilful piloting saved them from early disaster. After a period that seemed far longer than it actually was, they were well above the buildings and trees, and Brown glanced across at Alcock and noticed that the perspiration of acute anxiety was running down his face.

They wasted no time or fuel in circling around the airfield while striving for height but headed straight into the wind until they were at about 800 feet. Then they turned towards the sea and continued to climb at a leisurely rate, with engines throttled down. As they passed their airfield Brown leaned over the side of the machine and waved farewell to the small groups of mechanics and sightseers. Freddie Raynham, who had so sportingly loaned his airfield to Alcock and Brown and whose own mechanics had broken off their repair work to his machine to help manoeuvre the Vimy into position before take-off, must have looked on with mixed emotions. After all, with a bit more luck it might have been him heading out. Another man who would have been looking skywards as the Vimy passed over St John's was Major Fiske, who had arrived in the town that very day to begin searching for a suitable site for Boulton and Paul's Atlantic challenge. It turned out to be a wasted journey.

The Vimy, although loaded to the extent of about eleven pounds per square foot demonstrated its excellent lift capability, climbing satisfactorily, if slowly. Eight minutes passed before they had reached 1,000 feet.

As they passed over St John's and Cabot Hill towards Concepcion Bay the air was bumpy; not until they reached the coast and were away from the uneven contours of Newfoundland did it become calmer. The eddying wind, which was blowing behind them from almost due west with a strength of thirty-five knots, made it harder than ever to keep the machine on a straight course. Usually the twin-engine Vimy was a stable aircraft and not especially sensitive to atmospheric instability, but under the present conditions it lurched, swayed, and did its best to deviate, much as if it had been a little single-seater fighter.

They crossed the coast at 16:28 (Greenwich time), the altimeter then registering about 1,200 feet. Just before they left the land Brown let out the wireless aerial and tapped out on the transmitter key a message to Mount Pearl Naval Station: 'All well and started.' That was to be the only signal from Alcock and Brown for the entire crossing.

News of their departure was sent in a signal by Lieutenant Clements: 'Captain Alcock and Lieut. Brown left St John's, Newfoundland in a

Vickers-Vimy machine on a flight to England today, June 14, at 4:13pm, Greenwich Mean Time.'

Slowly but surely, Newfoundland slipped away beneath and behind them. As they continued to climb, the altitude flattened the landscape into a mosaic of St John's roofs, and then fields, woods and hills which finally gave way to the greyness of the Atlantic ocean. Behind them lay Newfoundland, and ahead in the far distance, Europe. In between there was nearly 2,000 miles of ocean. For the two men alone in the sky in their Vimy, there was little time to dwell on the vastness of the space ahead of them. As they settled into their flight routine Brown busied himself with his navigation instruments and charts, checking their position against the sun, horizon, sea-surface and time of day. He recalled afterwards: 'I felt a queer but quite definite confidence in our safe arrival over the Irish coast, based, I suppose, on an assured knowledge that the machine, the motors, the navigating instruments and the pilot were all first-class.'

He and Alcock even spent a few moments speculating what sort of reception they would get and what meal they would like to eat.

At last the Vimy shook itself free from the atmospheric disturbances over the land and settled into an even stride through the calmer spaces above the ocean. The westerly wind behind them, added to the power developed by the motors, giving them a speed along their course (as opposed to 'air-speed') of nearly 140 knots, some forty knots more than the Vimy's 'normal' cruising speed.

Visibility was fairly good during the first hour of the flight. Above, at a height of something between two and three thousand feet, a wide ceiling of clouds was made jagged at intervals by holes through which the blue sky could be glimpsed. Below, the sea was blue-grey and dull for the most part. Here and there the greyness was lifted by pools of sunlight that streamed through gaps in the cloud. Icebergs stood out prominently from the surface, in splashes of glaring white.

As the weather was still fair, Brown took the opportunity to get as many 'readings' as possible. Careful plotting of their course now would help them immeasurably if the weather turned bad.

Almost inevitably, the weather did take a turn for the worse, much worse. Towards evening they ran into an immense bank of fog that seemed to stretch right across the horizon, shutting off completely the surface of the ocean. The blue of the sea merged into a hazy purple, and then into the dullest kind of grey so that sky and sea became one grey mass. They were entering an area to the south-east of Newfoundland known as the Grand Banks. The mix of the warm currents of the Gulf Stream meeting colder northern currents often creates thick fogs. Hawker had encountered it and now it was the turn of Alcock and Brown.

The cloud screen above them also grew much thicker, and there were no more gaps in it. The occasional glints of sunlight on the wing-tips and struts no longer appeared. Brown, having taken one last reading before they were enveloped by the fog, was now unable to obtain observations on the sun, nor calculations of drift from the sea. For the next few hours he would have to rely on dead reckoning to get them to Ireland as best he could. As he had been diligent in taking readings when they were in good weather, Brown had a good fix from which to start. By constantly monitoring their speed and making slight adjustments to their course to allow for compass variations, he was able to keep them on a remarkably accurate course. It also required Alcock to fly as precisely as he could, keeping his speed as constant as possible and flying as straight and level as atmospheric conditions would allow.

Alcock meanwhile was having to cope with his own difficulties. With his vision of the horizon masked by fog it was almost impossible for him to keep the Vimy flying straight. Even in modern aircraft equipped with an array of sensitive instruments, 'blind flying' in such conditions still tests even the most experienced pilots. The Vimy had few instruments, and so keeping the aircraft as close as possible to Brown's course must have been mentally exhausting. Physically, the pilot had to 'fly' the Vimy all the time as it had no means of setting its trim which would have eased the need for Alcock to constantly make inputs via the control column. In a heavy aircraft this must have been physically tiring after several hours. The demands on Alcock were made harder as the fuel load got lighter as the Vimy would start to fly nose down, or up, depending on which tanks were emptied first.

As they flew through the wide layer of air sandwiched between fog and cloud, Brown began to jot down remarks for the log of the journey. At 17:20 he noted that they were at 1,500 feet and still climbing slowly, while the haze was becoming ever thicker and heavier.

They were now about three hours into their flight Brown leaned towards the wireless transmitter and began to send a message; but the small propeller on it snapped and broke away from the generator. Why remained a mystery, as careful examination, both at the time and after they landed, showed no defect. It meant they would have to continue their flight with the outside world oblivious to their fate. There would be no easy means of summoning assistance if they ditched into the heaving seas of the Atlantic. It also meant that Brown would not be able to confirm their position on his charts. Success was now their only option.

Although the battery heating their flying suits would eventually die without the generator, for now all was well in the Vimy's cockpit, the thrumming drone of the engines taking them ever eastwards into the approaching night.

For a time Alcock and Brown attempted short conversations through their cockpit radio. Its earpieces were under their fur helmets while a small transmitter was held against their throats. It was not a particularly comfortable system to wear for any length of time and at about six o'clock Alcock discarded his earpieces because they were too painful. For the rest of the flight they communicated in gestures and by scribbled notes, something made easier by sitting side by side.

Brown continued to keep the course by dead reckoning, taking into account height, compass bearing, strength of wind, and his previous observations. The wind varied quite a lot, and several times the nose of the Vimy swayed from the right direction so that he had to make rapid mental allowances for deviation. He wrote down any corrections to the course on slips of paper in his notebook, tearing them out and passing them to Alcock.

For example, the first was: 'Keep her nearer 120 than 140.'

The second informed him that the transmitter was useless: 'Wireless generator smashed. The propeller has gone.'

Throughout the evening they flew between a covering of unbroken cloud and a screen of thick fog which shut off the sea completely. Brown's scribbled comment to Alcock at 17:45 was: 'I can't get an obs. in this fog. Will estimate that same wind holds and work by dead reckoning.'

Despite the lack of anything to see outside the cockpit, the early evening was by no means dull. Just after 18:00 they were startled when the starboard engine started making a loud, rhythmic chattering, rather like the noise of machine-gun fire at close quarters. Immediately thoughts turned to the engine trouble which had caused Hawker and Grieve to crash in mid-Atlantic. They both looked anxiously for the cause.

It was not hard to find. A section of exhaust pipe had split away and was quivering in the rush of air like a reed. It began to glow red- then white-hot, and then, softened by the heat, it gradually crumpled up. Finally it was blown away, with the result that three cylinders were blowing their exhaust straight into the air. The chattering swelled into a loud, jerky thrum, much more prominent than the normal noise of a Rolls-Royce aero-engine. This settled down to a steady and continuous roar. There was nothing they could do about the broken exhaust pipe until they landed and so they accepted it as just a minor problem. Although the deafening roar was unpleasant, they soon became accustomed to it and settled back into the rhythm of their flight.

What was disconcerting for Brown was that he noticed a little flame licking out from the open exhaust. It was playing on one of the cross-bracing wires and had made it glow red-hot. The problem could be reduced by Alcock easing the throttle on the starboard engine, but this meant losing altitude, and at this stage of the flight they needed height.

For hours they flew. The fog seemed never ending. They had become accustomed to the insistent roar of the engine. In fact the noise made the solitude seem somehow more normal. As Brown observed afterwards: 'The long flight would have been dreadful had we made it in silence; for, shut off as we were from sea and sky, it was a very lonely affair. At this stage the spreading fog enveloped the Vimy so closely that our sheltered cockpit suggested an isolated but by no means cheerless room.'

At around 19:00 they rose through a layer of clouds at about 2,000 feet. Moisture began to condense on goggles, dial glasses and wires. As he could not see, Alcock removed his goggles, and Brown only used his to protect his eyes in the slipstream when leaning over the side of the fuselage to take observations.

Emerging into the air above the clouds, Brown looked upward, and found another stretch of cloud-bank still higher, at 5,000 feet. It meant they remained cut off from the sun. Still guided only by dead reckoning, Alcock and Brown continued to fly the Vimy along the airway between a white ceiling of cloud and a white carpet of cloud.

Several hours had passed since Brown had last been able to take a reading and so he was anxious for an opportunity to take further observations either of the sun or of the stars. This would enable him to check that they were still travelling on the right course. At 19:40 he handed Alcock the following note: 'If you get above clouds, we will get a good fix tonight, and hope for clear weather tomorrow. Not at any risky expense to engines though. We have four hours yet to climb.'

The altimeter was then registering 3,000 feet.

All this while Brown had listened occasionally for wireless messages, as the receiver was still in working order. Every so often he would hear fragments of signals from passing ships not meant for them but reassuring all the same that they were not alone. Even that small sign of contact with life below cheered him mightily.

The current conditions meant giving their full attention to navigation and precise flying such as they could. Although they had packed food, there was little time to relax and eat. Instead they had to eat and drink in snatches, whenever they could. However, as they recorded later, neither of them felt hungry at any time during the sixteen hours of the flight, although now and then they felt the need of something to drink.

The food was packed into a little cupboard behind Brown's head on the left-hand side of the fuselage. At about 19:30 he thought Alcock might need some nourishment and so he reached in and passed him two sandwiches and some chocolate as well as uncorking the thermos flask. Rather than risk any loss of control, Alcock ate and drank using one hand while keeping the other on the control wheel.

As the sky to the east deepened into evening, they found themselves flying under a large gap in the upper layer of clouds. It was 20:30 and through the gap the sun still shone brightly, projecting the shadow of the Vimy onto the cloud layer beneath them, over which it darted and twisted, contracting or expanding according to the distortions on the cloud-surface.

The gaps in the cloud meant that Brown was able to maintain observation on the sun for some ten minutes. The calculations he was able to make showed that if they were still on the right course, the machine must be further east than was indicated by dead reckoning. From this he concluded that the strength of the wind must have increased rather than fallen off, as had been forecast in the report by the meteorologist back at St John's. This supposition was borne out by the buffeting which from time to time swayed the Vimy. Up until then their average speed had been 143 knots.

Despite the cramped conditions in the cockpit and their bulky flying suits, Brown was able to kneel on his seat and get his observations of the sun while looking between the port wings. He made use of the spirit level, as the horizon was invisible, and the sextant could therefore not be used.

Later he caught sight of the sea for a few brief moments, and at 21:15 wrote the following note to Alcock: 'Through a rather bad patch I have just made our ground speed 140 knots, and from the sun's altitude we must be much further east and south than I calculated.'

He continued to keep a log of their movements and observations, and at 21:20 made the following entry: 'Height 4,000 feet. Dense clouds below and above. Got one sun observation, which shows that dead reckoning is badly out. Shall wait for stars and climb. At 08:31 position about 49 deg. 31 minutes north, 38 deg. 35 minutes west.'

The clouds above remained constant, at a height of about 5,000 feet. Brown was eager to pass through them before the stars appeared; and at 21:30, when the light was fading, he scribbled another message to Alcock: 'Can you get above these clouds at, say, 60°? We must get stars as soon as poss.'

Alcock nodded and proceeded to climb as steeply as he dared. Twilight was now setting in, gradually but noticeably. Between the layers of cloud, the daylight, although never very good, had until then been strong enough to let Brown read the instruments and his chart. At ten o'clock this was no longer possible without artificial light. He switched on a tiny bulb which was placed so as to make the face of the compass clear in the dark, all the other fixed instruments were luminous. For his intermittent inspection of the engines he had to flash the electric torch over either side of the cockpit.

Ominously, the clouds, both above and below, grew denser and darker so that they became one nebulous mass. It became more and more difficult to judge how near to or how far from them they were. An entry in the log, made at 22:20, says: 'No observations, and dead reckoning apparently out. Could not get above clouds for sunset. Will wait check by stars.'

An hour later they had climbed to 5,200 feet. But still they found clouds above them. It was becoming more and more important that they continue to climb, so as to be above the cloud in time for some early observations on the stars.

It was now quite dark; and as the Vimy droned on their isolated way eastward and upward, nothing could be seen outside the cockpit except the inner struts, the engines, the vapour ejected through the exhaust pipes which glowed red, and portions of the wings, which glistened in the dim glimmer of the moon.

Brown was impatient to get sight of the moon, the Pole Star, or any other stars, the night-time friends of every navigator throughout history.

Midnight came and went amid sullen darkness, modified only by dim moonlight and the red mist that spurted from the engines' exhaust pipes.

By then they must have climbed to about 6,000 feet, although Brown's log shows no record of their height at this stage. Meanwhile they were still between the upper and lower ranges of cloud banks.

At 00:15 Alcock took the Vimy through the upper range, only to find a third layer of clouds, several thousand feet higher. This, however, was patchy and without continuity, so Brown was able to glimpse the stars from time to time.

At 00:25 he identified the star Vega through a gap to the north-east which shone very brightly high in the heavens, and the Pole Star. With their help, and that of a cloud horizon that was clearly defined in the moonlight not far below their level, he used the sextant to fix their position.

This he found was latitude 50° 7′ N and longitude 31° W, showing that they had flown 850 nautical miles at an average speed of 106 knots. They were still slightly to the south of the correct course, which Brown made known to Alcock in a note, with pencilled corrections for correcting the deviation.

Most of his dead reckoning calculations were short of their actual position because, influenced by meteorological predictions based on the weather reports at St John's, Brown had allowed for a falling off in the strength of the wind, and this had not happened.

Having found the stars and checked their position and direction, it was no longer important that Alcock keep the Vimy climbing. He had been nursing the Vimy's engines carefully, and to reduce the strain on them he let the machine lose height slowly. At 01:20 they were back down to 4,000 feet, and an hour later they had dropped another 400 feet. With clearer atmosphere, Alcock could relax a little as he had some sort of horizon on which to fix the Vimy's position.

The clouds overhead were still patchy, clusters of stars lightening the intervals between them. But the Vimy was once more flying through a sea of fog, which prevented effective observation. This Brown made known to Alcock in a message: 'Can get no good readings. Observation too indefinite.'

The moon was visible for about an hour and a half, radiating a misty glow over the semi-darkness and tinging the tips of the clouds with variations of silver, gold and soft red. Whenever directly visible it projected the moving shadows of the Vimy onto the clouds below.

Brown could see the moon by looking over the aeroplane's starboard wings. He tried to get a sight on it for latitude, but the horizon was still too undefined.

An aura of unreality seemed to surround them as they flew onward towards the dawn and Ireland. The strangeness of their surroundings seemed even more extravagantly fantastic because of the distorted ball of a moon, the weird half-light, the monstrous cloud shapes, the fog below and around them, the misty indefiniteness of space, and the changeless drone of the motors.

To keep his mind on the task in hand, Brown turned to the small food-cupboard at the back of the cockpit. Twice during the night they drank and ate in snatches, Alcock keeping a hand on the control column while using his other to take the sandwiches, chocolate and thermos flask, which Brown passed to him one at a time.

It was bitterly cold outside the cockpit, but inside was warm due to the protective windscreen, the nearness of the radiators, and their thick clothing. But they were far from comfortable as movement was all but impossible in the cramped cockpit. At least Brown was able to find some relief when he turned to inspect the engines with his torch. After several hours they were desperate to kick out, to walk, to stretch themselves. It must have been particularly uncomfortable for Alcock who never removed his feet from the rudder-bars.

It was extraordinary that during the sixteen hours of the flight neither Alcock nor Brown felt the least desire for sleep. During the war, pilots and observers on night bombing sorties often struggled to remain awake on the homeward journey as the tension of the operation eased away and the monotonous, never-varying hum of the motor caused drowsiness to set in—and this after only four to six hours of continuous flying. Probably, however, such tiredness was mostly a reaction and mental slackening after the object of their journeys—the bombing of a target—had been achieved. Alcock and Brown's own objective would not be achieved until they saw Ireland beneath them; and it could not be achieved unless they kept their every faculty concentrated on it all the time. It was this thought that kept them going during the long hours of flying.

As they flew on, they began to think about sunrise and the new day. They had been flying for over ten hours; and the next ten would bring success or failure. They had more than enough petrol to complete the long journey, for Alcock had treated the engines gently, never running them all out, but varying the power from half to three-quarter throttle. Their course seemed satisfactory, and it seemed that only the chance of an engine mishap, such as had befallen Hawker and Grieve, or of something entirely unforeseen could stop them now. Their luck had stayed with them and they could have been forgiven for starting to think they might complete this flight.

The blackness of the night sky was just beginning to lighten. It would soon be sunrise and the start of a new day, a day in which Alcock and Brown would make history. But just as the welcoming glow of sunrise began to announce the presence of the new day, it was suddenly snuffed out. They were at between 3,500 and 4,000 feet when they ran into a thick bank of fog that projected above the lower layer of cloud. This was not like the fog they had experienced over the Grand Banks but something altogether different.

All around was dense, drifting fog, which was so thick they could not even see the machine's wing tips or the end of the fuselage in front of them.

Such dense fog was entirely unexpected. Suddenly isolated from any external reference, they became disorientated and lost their sense of spatial awareness. For a moment the machine, left to its own devices, swung, pitched, and seemed to fly in any direction. A glance at the instruments made it obvious that they were not flying level but Alcock was now battling with the physiological disruption caused by spatial disorientation. There was a danger of crashing.

Their air speed crept up to ninety knots while Alcock wrestled to regain control of the machine. He pulled back the control column, but apparently the air speed meter was jammed, for although the Vimy must have nosed upwards, the reading remained at ninety. They stalled—that is to say their speed dropped below the minimum necessary for heavier-than-air flight. The machine hung motionless for a second, after which it heeled over and fell into what was either a spinning nosedive, or a very steep spiral.

The compass needle continued to revolve rapidly, showing that the machine was swinging as it dropped; but still hemmed in as they were by the thick fog, they could not tell how, or in which direction they were spinning.

Before Alcock could reduce the throttle, the roar of the motors seemed twice as loud as before, and instead of the usual 1,650 to 1,700 rpm, they were running at about 2,200 rpm. Alcock shut off the throttles, and the vibration ceased.

Apart from the changing levels marked by the altimeter, only the weight of their bodies against the seats indicated that the machine was falling. How and at what angle it was falling, they had no idea. Alcock tried to centralise the controls but failed because he had lost all sense of what was central. There wasn't a single aerobatic manoeuvre he did not try. Brown, more or less helpless at this moment, searched in every direction for an external sign, anything that would give them a fix, and saw nothing but thick cloud.

The altimeter registered heights that dropped ever lower and alarmingly lower—3,000, 2,000, 1,000, 500 feet. Brown realised with horror that they might hit the ocean at any moment if the altimeter's accuracy had been affected by differences between the barometric conditions of their present position and those of St John's where the instrument was set. Moreover, the cloud might stretch down to the surface of the ocean; in which case Alcock, having obtained no sight of the horizon, would be unable to counteract the spin in time.

Brown made ready for the worst, loosening his safety belt and preparing to at least save his notes of the flight. All precautions would probably have been of little use however, for had they fallen into the sea, there would have been little hope of survival. They were on a steep slant, and even had they escaped drowning when first submerged, the dice would be heavily loaded against the chance of rescue by a passing ship.

Just as these thoughts were chasing each other across Brown's mind, they left the cloud as suddenly as they had entered it. But they were now less than a hundred feet above the ocean. The surface did not appear below the machine, but, because the angle at which the aircraft was tilted, the sea seemed to stand up level, sideways to them.

Alcock looked at the ocean and the horizon and almost instantaneously regained his sense of equilibrium. With amazing dexterity he managed to manoeuvre the heavy, cumbersome Vimy into a safer position. Fortunately the Vimy manoeuvred well, and it responded rapidly to Alcock's action in centralizing the control column and rudder bar. He opened up the throttles. The motors came back to life, and the danger was past. They had been just seconds from almost certain death.

Later Alcock recounted the incident: 'The salty taste we noted later on our tongues was foam. In any case the altimeter wasn't working at that low height and I think that we were not more than 16 to 20 feet above the waters.'

When at last the machine swung back to the level and flew parallel with the Atlantic, their height was fifty feet. It appeared to them as if they could stretch down and almost touch the great white-caps that crested the surface. With the motors shut off they could actually *hear* the voice of the cheated ocean as its waves swelled, broke, and swelled again.

The compass needle, which had continued to swing, now stabilized itself and quivered towards the west, showing that the end of the spin had left them facing America. As they did not want to return to St John's, and really wanted to reach Ireland, Alcock turned the machine in a wide semi-circle and headed east, while climbing away from the ocean and towards the lowest clouds.

Alcock's skill and quick reaction had played a major part in saving them but there's no doubt that plain good luck also played its part, as had they not broken out of the cloud when they did, the Vimy would have plunged into the sea.

With the aircraft back under control they ploughed on, settling back into the flight routine that had been so violently interrupted. A gradual lightening of the sky to the east in front of them told them that it was sunrise. But all the light did was illuminate the dense clouds above and below. The sun itself was nowhere to be seen.

From what little they could see, it seemed they were flying in and out of dense patches of cloud; for every now and then they would pass through a white mountain, emerge into a small area of clear sky, and then be confronted with another enormous barrier of dense, seemingly never-ending cloud.

His inability to get a clear view of the sun was frustrating Brown in his attempts to get an update on their position. At three o'clock he had scribbled a note to Alcock: 'Immediately you see sun rising, point machine straight towards it, and we'll get compass bearings.'

Before they had left, Brown had already worked out a table of hours, angles and azimuths of the sun at its rising, to serve as a check on their position, but as things happened he had no choice but to resume navigation hoping luck and dead reckoning would guide them to their coveted goal.

Brown noted in the log that at 04:20 the Vimy had climbed to 6,500 feet and was above the lower range of clouds. The next three hours that followed sunrise he remembered chiefly as a period of being enveloped by clouds and ever more clouds. Soon, as they continued to climb, the aircraft was travelling through a mist of uniform thickness that completely shut off their range of vision outside a radius of a few yards from the wing-tips.

But now, as if they had not already faced enough challenges, Alcock and Brown faced a new hazard in the form of a spell of bad weather. It began as heavy rain before turning to snow. The downpour seemed to meet them almost horizontally, owing to the high speed of the machine.

The snow gave way to hail, mingled with sleet. The sheltered position of the cockpit, and the streamlining of the machine, kept them free from the downfall so long as they remained seated; but if one of them exposed a hand or a face above the windscreen's protection, it was bombarded by scores of painful stabs from the hailstones.

The freezing temperatures also brought new problems that seriously threatened their chances of making it to Ireland. The problem was that while they were flying blind in freezing fog, Alcock was completely dependent on his instruments to tell him whether he was flying straight and level or not. Ice was forming on the wings and fuselage making the Vimy harder to fly.

When they had reached a height of 8,800 feet, the radiator shutter and water temperature indicators began to cover with snow and ice. The air speed indicator was also not functioning properly once more. This relied on two intake tubes – a static and a pitot – to function properly and these were now getting blocked by ice particles. Although Alcock would have known if the Vimy was banking left or right through the seat of his pants, without the air speed indicator to tell him if he was losing or increasing speed, he would be unable to tell if he was climbing or the nose had dipped into a shallow dive. The second critical gauge was the rev-counter of which the Vimy had two, one for each engine. A sudden increase in revs would indicate the aircraft was diving and a sudden loss of revs would indicate that the aeroplane was climbing, perhaps steeply and in danger of stalling. With ice building up on the aircraft's surfaces, trim was being severely compromised, and unfortunately these instruments were mounted outside the cockpit and the build-up of snow and ice was making them unreadable. There was also the risk of icing on the carburettors. As Alcock could not take his hands off the controls for so much as a moment, it was up to Brown to try to clear these vital instruments of snow.

The only way to reach the frozen gauges was by climbing out of the cockpit and stretching out over the fuselage, while holding on to a strut for balance. For a man who still suffered from the war wound to his leg, this was a remarkable achievement. Having struggled to his feet, he experienced the sharp change from the comparative warmth of the cockpit to the biting, icy blast of cold air outside. He also had to contend with the rush of air from the slipstream which only added to his discomfort.

But having once got himself into position, he had no difficulty in reaching up and clearing the snow and ice with a knife. For several hours the snowstorm persisted, forcing Brown to repeat the whole process a number of times. He was safe as long as Alcock kept the machine straight and level, but the slightest jolt or bump could have pitched Brown out of the aircraft altogether.

They examined the state of the engines regularly, acutely aware that on them depended whether the next four hours would bring success or failure. In the meantime, they were still living for the moment; and although they were intensely glad that four-fifths of the ocean had been crossed, there was no time for idle speculation on what a safe arrival would mean to them. Perhaps surprisingly given the physical efforts both had been through during the stall and the snowstorm, neither of them was aware of the least sign of weariness, mental or physical.

When not struggling to clear the snow, Brown listened at the wireless receiver, but there were no messages for them from the beginning to the end of the flight. Any kind of communication with ship or shore would have been welcome, as a reminder that they were not out of touch with the world below. The complete absence of such contact made it seem that nobody cared about them and what they were attempting to achieve.

The entry that Brown scribbled in the log at 07:20 was that they had reached a height of 9,400 feet, and were still in drifting cloud, which was sometimes so thick that they could not even see the extremities of their aircraft. Snow was still falling, and the top sides of the wings were covered completely by a crust of frozen sleet presenting a new potential danger.

The sleet embedded itself in the hinges of the ailerons and jammed them so that for about an hour the machine had scarcely any lateral control. Fortunately the Vimy had plenty of inherent lateral stability and, as the rudder controls were never clogged by sleet, they were able to carry on, albeit with care.

It had been some hours since Brown had been able to get any readings for navigation and so Alcock continued to climb steadily to get above the seemingly interminable clouds and into clear sky. At five o'clock, when they were in the levels round about 11,000 feet, Brown caught the sun for a moment—just a pin-point glimmer through a cloud-gap. There was no horizon, but it was enough to enable him to get a reading with the help of his Abney spirit level.

This observation gave them a position close to the Irish coast. Yet he could not be sure of just where they were on the line on his chart indicated by it. They therefore remained at 11,000 feet until, at 07:20, he had definitely fixed the position line. Having done this, Brown scribbled the following message and handed it across to Alcock: 'We had better go lower down, where the air is warmer, and where we might pick up a steamer.'

Just as they started to nose downward, the starboard engine began to pop ominously, as if it were backfiring through one of its carburettors. Alcock throttled back while keeping the Vimy on a slow glide. The popping now ceased as the surrounding atmosphere warmed up.

By 08:00 they had descended from 11,000 to 1,000 feet, where the machine was still surrounded by heavy cloud. But the atmosphere was much warmer, and the ailerons, free of the build-up of ice, were operating again, although Alcock and Brown were now sitting in a puddle of water.

Alcock was feeling his way down very gently, not knowing whether the cloud extended to the ocean, nor at what moment the machine's undercarriage might touch the waves. He had loosened his safety belt and was ready to abandon ship if they hit the water. Brown was also worried about the danger of sudden immersion, as it was very possible that a change in barometric conditions could have made the altimeter show a false reading.

But once again, Alcock's piloting skills and a huge slice of good luck saved the day. They were just a few feet above the ocean when they emerged from the cloud base—a restless surface of dull grey. At once, Alcock opened up the throttles, and both engines responded. Evidently a short rest had been all that the starboard motor needed when it began to pop, as it now showed no further signs of trouble. He kept the Vimy at low altitude for the next forty minutes or so.

Brown now had plenty of opportunity to check their position. Reaching for the Drift Bearing Plate, and after observation on the ocean, he found that they were moving on a course 75 degrees true at 110 knots ground speed with a wind of 30 knots from the direction of 215 degrees true. He had been reckoning on a course of 77 degrees true, with calculations based on their position taken at midnight. Of course, he could see that they were north of the prescribed track. Still, they were not so far north as to miss Ireland altogether, which was all that mattered.

In his correction of the compass bearing, he could only really guess at the time when the wind had veered from its earlier direction. He had made the assumption that the northerly drift had existed ever since his sighting on the Pole Star and Vega during the night, and he reckoned that their position at eight o'clock would consequently be about fifty-four degrees N latitude, ten degrees thirty minutes W longitude. Taking these figures, and with the help of the navigation machine, which rested on his knees, he calculated that their course to Galway was about 125 degrees true. Allowing for variation and wind he therefore set a compass course of 170 degrees, and indicated to Alcock the necessary change in direction by means of a diagram and note: 'Don't be afraid of going S. We have had too much N. already.'

Alcock nodded and steered the Vimy around gently, until its compass showed a reading of 170 degrees.

If Brown's calculations were correct, then they were quite close to Ireland and journey's end. As they flew eastward, just below the lowest clouds and from 200 to 300 feet above the sea, they strained their eyes for a break in the monotonous vista of grey waves; but they could find not even a single ship.

Although neither of them felt hungry, they decided to have some breakfast at 08:00, partly to kill time and partly to take their minds from the rising excitement brought on by the hope that they might see land at any instant. Brown placed a sandwich, followed by some chocolate, in Alcock's left hand. His right hand always remained on the control lever and his feet on the rudder bar. At no time during the past sixteen hours had Alcock's hands and feet left the controls. This was a difficult achievement for such a long period. A rubber device, fitted to ease the strain, had proved to be useless. Elastic, linked to a turnbuckle, had been attached to the control lever and rudder bar; but in the hurry that preceded their departure from St John's, the elastic was cut too short. All the weight of the controls, therefore, were directly on the pilot.

The pressure on the controls was getting heavier the longer the flight went on as the Vimy now tended to sag downwards. It was now nose heavy as the centre of gravity had changed as the rear fuel tanks gradually emptied. Alcock now had to exert continuous backward pressure on the control lever to keep the nose up.

Brown had just screwed on the lids of the thermos flask, and was placing the remains of the food in the tiny cupboard behind his seat, when Alcock grabbed his shoulder and twisted him round. He beamed excitedly and pointed ahead and below. His lips were moving, but whatever he said was inaudible above the roar of the motors.

Brown followed the direction of Alcock's outstretched forefinger, and, barely visible through the mist, were two tiny specks of—*land*. For a moment, it hardly seemed true, but there they were. The time was 08:15 on June the 15th.

With a light heart, Brown put away his meticulously prepared charts and tables of calculation; wherever the compass needle pointed no longer mattered. His work as navigator of the flight was at an end. They could actually see journey's end.

Alcock flew straight towards the specks of land, which turned out to be two tiny islands—Eeshal and Turbot as they discovered afterwards.

Once they were above the islands the mainland was visible. Now all Alcock had to do was steer for the nearest point on it. The aircraft was still just underneath the clouds and flying at 250 feet, from which low height they could plainly see the white breakers foaming onto the shore. They crossed the coast of Ireland at 08:26.

But they were still uncertain of their exact position and so Brown suggested to Alcock that the best plan would be to find a railway line and follow it south. A few minutes later, however, the wireless masts of the Marconi station at Clifden came into view and gave the key to their position. As there did not seem to be anyone around, Brown fired two red flares from the Very pistol to try to attract attention. But as they seemed to go unnoticed from the ground, they circled over the village of Clifden, about two miles from the wireless station.

Although slightly off their course when they reached the coast, they were in the direct line of flight for Galway, which is where Brown had calculated they would land. Not far ahead they could see a cluster of hills, with their tops lost in low-lying clouds.

They could have continued to fly across Ireland, but the danger of running into high ground hidden from sight by the mist would have been too great. Alcock, therefore, decided to land.

If the sky had been clearer, they could easily have reached London before touching earth, for the tanks of the Vimy still contained enough fuel to keep the machine in the air for another ten hours. They had carried far more fuel than they needed in case they had lost their way over the ocean; there would have been a useful margin of time for cruising about in search of ships.

Having made up their minds to land at once, they searched below for a smooth stretch of ground. The most likely looking place in the area of Clifden was a smooth meadow near the wireless station. They circled around firing off Very lights but nobody seemed to notice the circling machine.

The Marconi station near Clifden is where Guglielmo Marconi established his first transatlantic telegraph station. It was from here that the world first heard of Alcock and Brown's success. (Unknown)

Alcock later said: 'We allowed this to the fact that no one expected us to make the flight, but now we were desperately in need of a place to land. We circled also over Clifden town and fired more signals but it seemed everyone was so soundly asleep that not even the drone of the engines could awaken them.'

They returned to the area by the radio station. Alcock shut off the engines as they glided towards it, heading into the wind. A few people had stirred out of the radio station at the noise of the aircraft's engines and were waving their arms as if trying to signal something. But Alcock and Brown were committed to landing.

At exactly the right moment, Alcock flattened out. The machine sank gently. As the wheels touched earth they began to run smoothly over the surface. Already Brown was indulging in the comforting reflection that the epic flight had ended with a perfect landing. Then, so softly as not to be noticed at first, the front of the Vimy tilted inexplicably, while the tail rose. Suddenly the craft stopped with an unpleasant squelch, tipped forward, shook itself, and remained poised on a slant, with its fore-end buried in the ground, as if trying to stand on its head.

Brown reached out a hand and arm just in time to save a nasty bump when the impact threw him forward. As it was, he only stopped a jarring collision with the help of his nose. Alcock had braced himself against the rudder control bar. The pressure he exerted against it to save himself from falling actually bent the straight bar almost into the shape of a horse-shoe.

What they had assumed was a smooth meadow was in fact Derrygimla Bog. The wheels had dug in causing the tail of Vimy to buck up in the air:

> It seemed an inglorious end to the first non-stop transatlantic flight. It was pitiful to see the distorted shape of the aeroplane that had brought us from America, as it sprawled in an ungainly manner over the sucking surface, its nose and lower wings crumpled and buried deep in the bog, its tail sticking up sixteen feet in the air.

The empty cockpit in front which was used by the observer in the Vimy bomber version was badly bent; but, being made of steel, it did not collapse. Quite possibly, this saved the lives of Alcock and Brown.

The leading edge of the lower wing was bent in some places and smashed in others, the fuel connections had snapped, and four of the propeller blades were buried in the ground, although none were broken.

The crumpled nose of the Vimy shows that Alcock and Brown were lucky to walk away from their crash landing in Ireland. It is perhaps fortunate that they had the front skid removed. (BAE Systems)

They had landed at 08:40 after being in the air for sixteen hours and twelve minutes. The flight from coast to coast, on a straight course of 1,680 nautical miles, lasted only fifteen hours and fifty-seven minutes, their average speed being 105 to 106 knots. For this relatively rapid performance, a strong following wind was largely responsible.

As a result of the connections between tank and carburettor being fractured, fuel began to swill into the rear cockpit while they were still inside it. Very fortunately the fuel did not ignite. Alcock had taken care to switch off the current on the magnetos as soon as he realised that a crash was imminent, so that electric sparks would not start a fire.

They scrambled out as best they could and lost no time in retrieving the mail bag and their instruments. The fuel spilled out rapidly, and it was impossible to withdraw the chart and the Baker navigating machine before they had been damaged.

Brown then fired two white flares from the Very pistols, as a signal for help. Almost immediately a small party, composed of officers and men belonging to the military detachment at Clifden, approached from the wireless station:

'Anybody hurt?' someone called when they arrived within shouting distance.

'No.'

'Where you from?'—this when they had helped us to clear the cockpit.

'America.'

Somebody laughed politely although they clearly did not believe them.

Evidently nobody took the comment seriously at first. Even a mention of their names meant nothing to them, and they remained unconvinced until Alcock showed them the mail bag from St John's. Their disbelief turned to surprise accompanied by spontaneous cheers and many painful handshakes. Guiding them carefully out of the bog they were led to the officers' mess for yet more congratulations and hospitality, a foretaste of what their lives would be like over the coming months. Some boys rushed up to see what was going on. Alcock tossed them an orange from their rations with the words:

'Have an orange from America. I was there yesterday, and I am the first man in Europe ever to say that!'

Getting out of the bog was far from easy, weighed down by their thick flying suits and heavy boots. Suddenly, the tension of the flight now behind them, Alcock and Brown discovered an intense sleepiness. Indeed, Brown said later that he was so fatigued he could easily have let himself lose consciousness while standing upright.

They lurched as they walked due to the stiffness that resulted from having sat in the tiny cockpit for nearly seventeen hours. Alcock, who during the whole period had kept his feet on the rudder bar and one hand on the control lever, would not admit to anything worse than a desire to stand up for the rest of his life—or at least until he could sit down painlessly. Brown's hands were very unsteady. His mind was quite clear on matters relating to the flight, but hazy on extraneous subjects. After having listened so long to the loud-voiced hum of the Rolls-Royce motors, made louder than ever by the broken exhaust pipe on the starboard side, they were both very deaf and their ears would not stop ringing.

However, Brown is reported to have said to Alcock:

'What do you think of that for fancy navigating?'

'Very good,' was the reply, upon which they shook hands.

When they arrived at the wireless station their first act was to send telegrams to Vickers, the London *Daily Mail*, and to the Royal Aero Club, confirming their arrival:

> Landed Clifden, Ireland at 8:40am, Greenwich mean time, June 15; Vickers-Vimy Atlantic machine. Leaving Newfoundland coast 4:28pm (GMT), June 14. Total time 16 hours 12 minutes. Instructions awaited.

A little later in that morning Brown was able to send a cable to his fiancée Kathleen Kennedy:

> Landed Clifden Ireland safely this morning. Will be with you soon. Teddy.

A reply came later in the day:

> Magnificent – never doubted your success. Wire when leaving for Brooklands. Will meet you there. Micki

It was an important formality that their arrival was validated. Major R.H. Mayo, the Royal Aero Club's representative, was in Dublin at the time and as soon as he received word he managed to get a lift in an aeroplane and car to get across to the other side of the country in double-quick time with the Irish correspondent of the *Daily Mail* for company. While they awaited his arrival, Alcock and Brown were able to enjoy a well-earned breakfast. After checking the seals, Major Mayo was happy to give official confirmation of Alcock and Brown's achievement in a message to the Royal Aero Club in London:

> The official time of arrival in Ireland (crossing the coast) was 9:25 British Summer Time, actual landing time 9:40am BST. I have examined the machine and found everything in order.

With the formalities over, Alcock and Brown began to remove the instruments and prepare for their journey back to London.

Later that day they were driven to Galway with a representative of the *Daily Mail*. For Brown it was a strange but welcome change to see solid

124

The crash landing in an Irish bog seemed an ignominious end after such an epic flight. (BAE Systems)

On-lookers soon ventured out from Clifden to see Vimy. Guards had to be positioned to protect the Vimy from further damage. (BAE Systems)

objects flashing past them, instead of miles upon monotonous miles of drifting, cloudy fog.

They were both desperately tired and needed sleep. But word of their achievement had already overtaken them and soon crowds were gathering.

The Vimy suffered considerable damage in the crash-landing. (BAE Systems)

Every time they stopped, they had to answer the same questions. It was difficult for them to answer with anything other than short perfunctory responses.

A reception had been prepared at Galway; but their hosts, realising how tired they must be, considerately made it a short and informal affair. Afterwards they slept for the first time in over forty hours.

Telegrams began to flood in, including one from the King:

> THE King was delighted to receive the welcome announcement that Captain Alcock and Lieut. Brown have safely landed in Ireland after their Transatlantic flight. His Majesty wishes you to communicate at once with these officers, and to convey to them the King's warmest congratulations on the success of their splendid achievement.

And from Prime Minister David Lloyd George:

> Heartiest congratulations to you and Lieut. Brown on your audacious and successful flight. It is a splendid achievement.

I am especially delighted that two British officers who fought in the War should have been the first to link Europe and America in a single non-stop flight.

And from Lord Northcliffe:

My dear Alcock, —

A very hearty welcome to the pioneer of direct Atlantic flight. Your journey with your brave companion, Whitten Brown, is a typical exhibition of British courage and organizing efficiency.

Just as in 1913, when I offered the prize, I felt that it would soon be won, so do I surely believe that your wonderful journey is a warning to cable monopolists and others to realise that within the next few years we shall be less dependent upon them unless they increase their wires and speed up. Your voyage was made more quickly than the average Press message of 1919. Moreover, I look forward with certainty to the time when London morning newspapers will be selling in New York in the evening, allowing for the difference between British and American time, and *vice versa* in regard to New York evening journals reaching London next day. Then we shall no longer suffer from the danger of garbled quotations due to telegraphic compression.

Then, too, the American and British peoples will understand each other better as they are brought into closer daily touch.

Illness prevents me from shaking you by the hand and personally presenting the prize. But I can assure you that your welcome will be equal to that of Hawker and his gallant American compeer, Read, whose great accomplishment has given us such valuable data for future Atlantic work. I rejoice at the good augury that you departed from and arrived at those two portions of the British Commonwealth, the happy and prosperous Dominion of Newfoundland and the future equally happy and prosperous Dominion of Ireland.

Although the prize fund had been put up by the *Daily Mail*, only a handful of papers published Sunday editions and only one was able to get an evening edition out on time, *The Evening Telegram*. Under the headline 'Great British Air Triumph' it carried a brief comment from Alcock:

> We are tired of this, alone in the fog and drizzle, sometimes discovering that I was flying upside down. The wireless propeller blew off soon after leaving St John's, and we were much jammed by strong wireless signals not intended for us.

The next morning, Alcock and Brown awoke to find themselves in a wonderland that seemed a long way from reality. Even getting up at 7 am after nine hours of sleep seemed strange, as they were still acclimatised to Newfoundland time which was five hours behind. Alcock would later note that they felt hungry at the 'wrong times' – perhaps the first person to describe the symptoms of what we today call jet lag. This difficulty of adjustment to the sudden change in time lasted for several days. Brown correctly predicted: 'Probably it will be experienced by all passengers travelling on the rapid trans-ocean air services of the future—those who complete a westward journey becoming early risers without effort, those who land after an eastward flight becoming unconsciously lazy in the mornings, until the jolting effect of the dislocation wears off, and habit has accustomed itself to the new conditions.'

After a good breakfast there began a succession of congratulatory ovations which Alcock and Brown were totally unprepared for. First came a reception from the town of Galway, involving many addresses and the presentation of a memento in the form of Claddagh rings, which had historical connections with a landing on the coast of Ireland nearby by vessels of the Spanish Armada. It was a taste of things to come now that their story was all over the pages of the world's newspapers.

The *Daily Mail* had finally got its story, carrying the first account from Alcock:

> We have had a terrible journey. The wonder is that we are here at all. We scarcely saw the sun or the moon or the stars. For hours we saw none of them. The fog was very dense, and at times we had to descend to within 300 feet of the sea.
>
> For four hours the machine was covered in a sheet of ice caused by frozen sleet; at another time the sleet was so dense and for a few seconds my speed indicator did not work, and for a few seconds it was very alarming.

We looped the loop I do believe and did a very steep spiral. We did some very comic 'stunts', for I had no idea of the horizon.

The winds were favourable all the way: north-west and at times, south-west. We said in Newfoundland we would do the trip in sixteen hours, but never thought we should. An hour and a half before we saw land we had no certain idea of where we were, but we believed we were at Galway or thereabouts. Our delight in seeing Eeshal Island and Turbot Island was great. People did not know who we were when we landed, and thought we were scouts on the lookout for the 'Vimy'.

We encountered no unforeseen conditions. We did not suffer from cold or exhaustion except when looking over the side; then the sleet chewed bits out of our faces. We drank coffee and ale and ate sandwiches and chocolate.

The flight has shown that the Atlantic flight is practicable, but I think it should be done not with an aeroplane or seaplane, but with a flying boat. We had plenty of reserve fuel left, using only two thirds of our supply.

The only thing that upset me was to see the machine at the end get damaged. From above, the bog looked like a lovely field, but the machine sank into it up to the axle and fell over on to her nose.

The warm-hearted crowd that they found waiting at Galway Station both amazed and daunted them. They were grateful for their loud appreciation but felt that they were barely able to respond to it adequately. Flowers were offered, and they met the vanguard of the autograph hunters. They signed their names hundreds of times during the journey to Dublin— on books, cards, old envelopes and scraps of paper of every shape and every state of cleanliness. They struggled to understand why so many people wanted their autographs, when three days earlier few people had heard of them. Somehow the non-stop flight across the Atlantic meant as much to the men, women and children that crowded every station on the route to Dublin as it did to Alcock and Brown, in the same way that the first moon landing became a shared experience. The cheers were not so much for Alcock and Brown as for the spirit of adventure and the idea that anything was possible, that mankind could conquer the frontiers and open up new horizons.

At one station, where a military band played their train in and out again, a wooden model of an aeroplane was presented to Alcock by a schoolboy. When they finally reached Dublin, Alcock and Brown passed with difficulty through the welcoming crowds and drove towards the Automobile Club in separate cars. But when Brown reached the relative sanctuary of the Club, there was no sign of Alcock. They waited and waited, and finally sent out scouts to search for him. They came back with the news that he had been kidnapped and taken to Commons in Trinity College. After celebrating his achievement in suitable style, Alcock was then 'released' to join Brown at the Royal Aero Club.

Landing at Holyhead next morning, they were welcomed back to England by Reginald 'Rex' Pierson, designer of the Vimy, Captain Vickers of the famous firm that built it, and by Claude Johnson of Rolls-Royce. Scenes all along the line to London were a magnified repetition of those that had greeted them from Galway to Dublin. A *Times* reporter captured the atmosphere when the two 'sons of Manchester' stopped at Chester for a reception:

> Amid the cries the voice of Lancashire seemed to dominate that of Cheshire and suggested that people had travelled from Manchester to see the newly famous sons of their city. 'Good old Lancashire' shouted a man of the merchant class. 'Ay, good owd Lankersheer!' echoed a railwayman. 'Manchester again!' cried another enthusiast. Captain Alcock stepped out onto the platform, and Lieutenant Brown, after a little hesitation, followed him.

At Crewe they were met by an even more boisterous reception:

> In Crewe station there was yet another crowd, which quickly found the saloon and insisted on the airmen leaving the train during the halt. Shout clashed with shout, 'Good luck as long as you live!' called one man. 'Which is Alcock? He's my namesake!' said another. A burly worker stretching his hand over the medley of others exclaimed, 'Put one in here, Mr Alcock, and God bless you!' Women and men struggled together to touch the Captain and Lieutenant – both for preference – and imperative demands from the rear end ended in a kind of slow procession past the saloon door. Suddenly, an Australian

soldier called to a porter 'Up with him', and Lieutenant Brown was lifted shoulder high so that all the people could see and cheer him. Another soldier with assistance hoisted up Captain Alcock. Then the whistle blew, and the throng had to let them go. Both men now were beginning to be a little exhausted by their reception and expressed some nervousness about what would happen in London.

For two modest men unaccustomed to being in the limelight, these kinds of receptions must have become something of an ordeal. Brown was quite a shy man. The report continued:

> At Rugby Lieutenant Brown's shyness must have finally got the better of him, for instead of leaving the train to greet Miss Kathleen Kennedy, his fiancée, who with her father, Major D H Kennedy, had travelled to meet him, he remained in the saloon, and Miss Kennedy, pretty, slim, tall and daintily dressed, stepped into the carriage. Captain Alcock promptly jumped out to face the enthusiastic crowd and write more autographs, and then before the train left, brought Lieutenant Brown and Miss Kennedy arm in arm to the door to share the cheers.

Finally, when they arrived at London's Euston Station just after six o'clock in the evening, it was estimated that a crowd of 250,000 was waiting to greet them. One of the first to welcome them was Harry Hawker. As they made their way by open Rolls-Royce to the Royal Aero Club in Clifford Street, they were mobbed by crowds throwing confetti and flowers. As he arrived Alcock handed over the small linen bag he had kept with him all the way from Ireland. It contained the small bundle of 197 letters that Dr Robinson, the postmaster in Newfoundland, had entrusted to the airmen before they left. They were immediately rushed to the nearest post office to be franked and passed on for delivery. Air mail stamps had yet to be invented. A new record for mail delivery had been set, although Alcock expressed his regret that it had not been possible to fly direct to London with the letters.

After the speeches were made, inside the clamour from outside to see the airmen was so great that they managed to squeeze onto a small balcony of the Royal Aero Club. Alcock graciously acknowledged the crowd with the words, 'Here we are. I want to thank you for your reception. The flight we made was not so wonderful as the reception you have given us.' Later that evening they separated, Alcock to see a big prize fight, Brown to visit his fiancée. The prize money would mean he could now afford to marry her.

The plaudits poured in from, among others, US President Wilson and Prime Minister Lloyd George. The next day, they were guests of honour at a reception held at the Vickers works at Weybridge with all the men and women who had built the transatlantic Vimy. This was followed by the formal reception held by the *Daily Mail* in London's Savoy Hotel on Friday, 20 June. Here Winston Churchill, who was then Secretary of State for War, presented them with their prize. As well as Lord Northcliffe's ten thousand pounds, the fund had been boosted by a further two thousand guineas (£2,200) from the Ardath Tobacco Company and one thousand pounds from a Mr Lawrence R. Phillips for being the first British subjects to fly the Atlantic.

In passing over the cheque, Churchill said: 'I do not know what we should admire the most – their audacity, their determination, their skill, their science, their Vickers Vimy aeroplane, their Rolls-Royce engines or their good fortune.'

It was a combination of all these things that had brought their success, and in recognition of this, Alcock and Brown asked for two thousand pounds to be shared by their support team.

Winston Churchill presented Alcock and Brown with their prize cheque. (BAE Systems)

The cheque was presented to the flyers at a special lunch at London's Savoy hotel. (BAE Systems)

The honours continued to mount. The United States conferred on them the Congressional Medal of Honour. They were made Knight Commanders of the British Empire, and then a few days later, following an audience with the King, they left Windsor Castle as Sir John Alcock and Sir Arthur Whitten Brown.

Throughout the rest of June and July, Alcock and Brown were caught up in a whirlwind of galas, presentations and celebration lunches and dinners offering menus with outlandish names like: Oeufs Pochés Alcock, Suprême de Sole à la Brown, Poulet de Printemps à la Vickers Vimy, Salade Clifden, Surprise Britannia, Gateau Grand Succès.

Eventually, however, the pressure on their time began to ease and Alcock was able to return to his test flying duties at Vickers despite his newfound wealth and celebrity.

On 29 July 1919, Sir Arthur Whitten Brown married Kathleen Kennedy in London with Sir John Alcock as a witness. They then took an extended honeymoon trip through America where Sir Arthur and Lady Whitten Brown were fêted wherever they went.

For three months between May and July 1919, Alcock and Brown were the stars who shone brightest. Their Atlantic crossing was the first of several feats of aviation that enthralled people around the world. First there was the R-34 airship, that not only crossed the Atlantic east to west but then flew the return flight. Next there was the flight to Australia by two Australian pilots, Ross and Keith Smith, with engineers Wally Shiers and Jim Bennett.

As the world headed towards another peaceful Christmas it seemed that aviation showed the way forward, that it could bring nations together. For the first time since before the war, Paris was going to host a major exhibition of aircraft and aero engineering in the Grand Palais. Vickers were eager to capitalise on the reputation gained as a result of the transatlantic and Australia flights and had decided to exhibit the all-new Viking amphibian. The plan was to fly the Viking to Paris and land it on the River Seine directly outside the exhibition halls. The aircraft was powered by a single Rolls-Royce Falcon engine mounted in a 'pusher' configuration. It could seat up to five in an enclosed cabin.

But first Alcock had an important duty to perform. The 'Atlantic' Vimy had been retrieved from the bog in western Ireland and repaired. In recognition of Alcock and Brown's achievement it was decided that it

Ross and Keith Smith's Vimy. (BAE Systems)

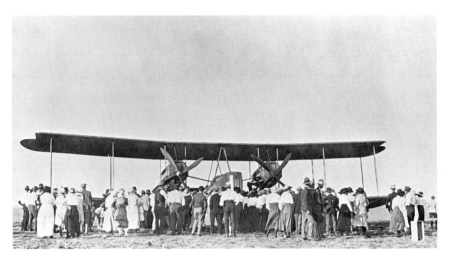

Crowds swarm around the Australia flight Vimy. (BAE Systems)

G-EAOU 'God 'Elp All Of Us' ready for the flight to Australia in December 1919. (BAE Systems)

The Rolls Royce Falcon powered Vickers Viking flying boat that crashed near Rouen, France killing Sir John Alcock on December 18, 1919. (BAE Systems)

should be preserved for the nation in London's Science Museum. As Brown was still in America, it fell to Alcock to perform the official handing over ceremony on 15 December. The aircraft is still on display to this day.

December 18 dawned shrouded in a thick fog. The addition of rain and strong winds meant that ordinarily this would be a 'no-flying' day. Alcock was due to take the Viking prototype down to Paris but it looked like the weather would make the journey impossible. Certainly, colleagues at the factory were trying their hardest to talk him out of it.

While they waited to see if the weather might clear just enough, Alcock had time to reflect on a year that was almost done. What a year it had been! Almost exactly a year ago he had stood on the dock at Dover waiting to be 'processed' after months in captivity as a prisoner of war. He stood there with little more to his name than the clothes he was standing in, but he was a man with a plan and he was eager to turn it into reality. Now he was a knight of the realm, he had money, he was popular and he had a job he loved.

Daylight hours are short at this time of year and although the weather showed little sign of improvement, Alcock left without a navigator.

The weather over the English Channel was blustery and the fog as thick over the Normandy coast as it had been at Brooklands. It seems that Alcock

Alcock and Brown's Vimy was brought back from Ireland and repaired. Sir John Alcock presented the aircraft to the Science Museum in December 1919. (Hugh Llewelyn)

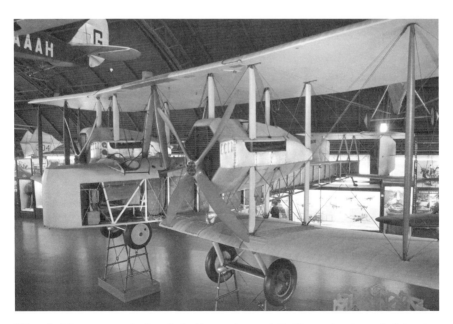

When the Vimy was repaired, cockpit side panels were left off exposing the cockpit interior. (Hugh Llewelyn)

may have decided to see if he could get below the cloud base and try to find a town or railway line he could identify.

At about one o'clock in the afternoon, a farmer named Pelletier was working in a field at Cottévrard near Rouen. The noise of the aircraft approaching out of the mist made him look up and, in his words, he saw a big plane 'become unsteady, make a big sway and fall to earth'. The accident was also witnessed by a local priest, Father Cellpiur.

It would appear that Alcock was looking for somewhere to land as he feared the weather would be worse inland. The weather was indeed perfectly clear in Paris. As he was making a final approach, he clipped a tree, but he may also have been surprised by the presence of a wire fence and, not wanting to damage an aircraft that was due to go on display, tried to lift the nose enough to carry him over, which induced a stall. The aircraft went in nose first, slamming Alcock into the windscreen and fracturing his skull.

The farmer and Father Cellpiur found the badly injured Alcock unconscious in the cabin. He was wearing a civilian suit and from papers he was carrying as well as the engraved watch on his wrist Pelletier realised who the casualty was.

With the help of another farm worker, Alcock was extracted from the wreckage and carried to the farmhouse. But it was a remote location and finding help was going to take time. British army vehicles often passed and so the worker was sent up to the road in the hope that he could flag a passing convoy down. Unfortunately, no trucks were passing, but they managed to get word to the No 6 British General Hospital at Rouen. Doctors were sent out immediately and Alcock was brought back to the hospital where they attempted to relieve the injury to his skull. But it was to no avail and Alcock died soon after.

A military escort transported his body from Le Havre back across the Channel. At London's Waterloo Station they were met by Alcock's parents and representatives of Vickers. It was Christmas Day. His funeral was held on 27 December at Manchester's South Cemetery.

The King's message delivered by Lieutenant Colonel Clive Wigram to his parents was as follows:

> The King desires me to express his deep sympathy with you in the untimely and tragic death of your distinguished son, whose name will ever occupy an honoured place in the roll of British airmen who never spared themselves in order to uphold the honour of their country. It was with pleasure His Majesty

recently decorated your son for his great feat in crossing the Atlantic, and the King feels that the early close in the prime of manhood of so valuable a life is an irreparable loss.

The news of his death spread far and wide beyond the world of aviation, such was Alcock's reputation, but they also reveal one or two disturbing facts.

Each day, Sir John Alcock had been taking new machines from the Weybridge factory to different parts of the country. Only the week before his fatal crash, Sir John had had a narrow escape while attempting to land in poor weather near Chelmsford. He skimmed over a railway embankment, under some telephone wires before crashing through a hedge. Both Sir John and his two passengers escaped unhurt. Secondly, Sir John was suffering from malaria-like symptoms probably picked up from his time as a prisoner of war, which according to his mother would come on very quickly and without warning. He had already experienced two attacks since the Atlantic crossing, and they were debilitating enough to force him to stay in bed for two or three days at a time. Given that he was doing a lot of flying, perhaps with an underlying illness, it is possible Sir John's judgment was not as sharp as it had been in the past.

One man who never really got over his friend's death was Sir Arthur Whitten Brown. He was still in America when he got word of Sir John's death, and he never flew again. Later he worked for Metropolitan-Vickers, the company that had once been British Westinghouse. In 1923 he was appointed chief representative for Metropolitan-Vickers in the Swansea area. During the Second World War Brown served in the Home Guard as a Lieutenant Colonel, before resigning his commission in July 1941, rejoining the RAF and working in Training Command instructing in navigation. His health deteriorated and by mid-1943 he had to give up RAFVR and ATC commitments on medical advice.

Brown's only son, Arthur (known as Buster), was killed on the night of 5/6 June 1944, aged 22, while serving with the RAF as a Flight Lieutenant. His aircraft, a De Havilland Mosquito VI, NT122, 605 Squadron, crashed in Holland. Buster was buried at Hoorn general cemetery. The death of his only son affected Brown badly.

By 1948 Brown's health had further deteriorated, although he was allowed to undertake restricted duties as general manager for Metropolitan-Vickers at the Wind Street offices.

Brown died in his sleep on 4 October 1948 from an accidental overdose of Veronal, a sleeping sedative, aged 62. Kathleen, his wife, died in May 1952, aged 56.

RACE ACROSS THE ATLANTIC

In the foreword to his account of their Atlantic crossing, Brown concluded:

> We have realized that our flight was but a solitary fingerpost to the air-traffic—safe, comfortable and voluminous—that in a few years will pass above the Atlantic Ocean; and even had the winning of the competition brought us no other benefits, each of us would have remained well content to be pioneers of this aerial entente which is destined to play such an important part in the political and commercial friendship between Great Britain and America.

And what of the other Atlantic challengers? Harry Hawker suffered a haemorrhage while flying a Nieuport Goshawk practising for a flying display at Hendon on 12 July 1921. He died in the ensuing crash but not before founding one of the greatest names in aviation: Hawker Aircraft Limited

Freddy Raynham finished rebuilding his 'Raymor' and made a successful test flight on 14 July. On 17 July he decided to make his Atlantic bid even though he knew there was no prize fund. With Lieutenant Charles Biddlecombe as his navigator, they taxied out onto the Quidi Vidi runway. This time he got a little further, but the weight of the extra fuel was too much for the little aircraft and it sagged into the ground. Fortunately Raynham and Biddlecombe were able to scramble out uninjured.

After the crash, Raynham decided to call it a day on the Atlantic attempt and returned to England where he became test pilot for his old friends Hawker and Sopwith in their new company.

The Handley Page entry suffered an equally inglorious conclusion to its efforts. Although there was every intention of making an attempt to beat the time set by Alcock and Brown, a practice flight on 18 June showed up a problem with the direction-finding wireless system. The problem was found to be the proximity of so many wires running through the airframe, causing interference.

With arch rivals Vickers winning the honours for being first across the Atlantic, Handley Page decided to make a demonstration flight to New York in the hope that this might produce orders for a civilian version of the V/1500. But on 5 July the aircraft was forced to make a crash landing in Parrsboro, Nova Scotia. Throughout the summer, the aircraft was repaired and continued its journey to New York, carrying the first air mail and passengers from Canada to the United States. There followed a number of other record-breaking flights before Major Brackley returned to England to become Chief of the Air Department at Handley Page Transport.

The following year he was an entrant in the London to Cape Town air race. This time, he was flying a Handley Page O/400, but once again he was beaten by a Vickers Vimy after he crashed near Khartoum with engine trouble.

Brackley died in a swimming accident in Rio de Janeiro on 15 November 1948.

Although Vickers had been reluctant to enter the Atlantic competition, the success proved that the Vimy was a good design. Its reputation was advanced even further when on 10 December 1919 a Vimy piloted by Australians Ross and Keith Macpherson Smith touched down on a race course in Darwin, becoming the first aircraft to fly to Australia. Twenty-eight days earlier they and two crew, Wally Shiers and Jim Bennett had left London, aiming to win a £10,000 prize put up by the Australian government. During their epic journey they encountered all manner of problems that tested both aeroplane and crew to the limit. But thanks to the ingenuity of the mechanics, aviator skill and the durability of the Vimy, they were able to overcome the setbacks and claim the prize which they divided equally amongst the four of them. Their journey had taken a flying time of 135 hours.

Aerial view of the HP V1500 'Atlantic' in flight on its way to New Jersey. (A Flying History)

Vimy G-EAOU Australia Flight group photo of crew in front of aircraft – Capt R Smith, Lt K Smith, Sgt JM Bennet, Sgt WH Shiers. (BAE Systems)

The following year two South African pilots, Pierre van Ryneveld and Quintin Brand, took off from Brooklands on 4 February in an attempt to win a new prize put up by the *Daily Mail* to be the first to fly from London to Cape Town. In 1920, many of the surveys of the continent were crude and communications were limited to a few thinly spread outposts. There were, of course, no airfields and the flight was to prove beyond the capabilities of what was, after all, First World War technology. The flight tested the aeroplane to the limit as the high temperatures they encountered during daytime created violent turbulence forcing them to fly at night. They also had to struggle with overheating engines, and just south of Cairo the aircraft was damaged beyond repair while attempting a crash landing. The engines were salvaged and sent down the River Nile by boat to be installed in a second Vimy. On 22 February they continued their journey, covering over 1,000 miles to Khartoum by following the railway. At Bulawayo their luck ran out. After topping off with more fuel the Vimy just could not get airborne, and crashed. The two men and their cat escaped with light injuries but it was the end of the Vimy. The rest of the journey was completed in an Airco DH 9. Although they were no longer able to claim the *Daily Mail* prize, they had succeeded in opening up African skies to air travel.

Pierre van Ryneveld (L) and C.J. Quintin Brand (R) stand in front of the 'Silver Queen' before their flight from London to Cape Town. (*Flight*)

The Vimy was converted into a very successful transport. (BAE Systems)

All three flights – the Transatlantic, Australia and South Africa – had used the original bomber version of the Vimy. In April 1919 a new 'civilian' version flew from its Joyce Green factory near Dartford. It had a wider fuselage so that it could carry up to ten passengers. In RAF service the Commercial became the Vernon and was its first dedicated troop transport.

In 1994 a replica Vimy began the first flight of what was to be three epic journeys. (Leading Edge)

Following the Australia flight, the Vimy replica's engines were replaced before the South Africa flight in 1999. (Leading Edge)

In 1994, a replica Vimy was built and used to recreate all three flights. The Transatlantic flight was flown on 2-3 July 2005 with Steve Fossett and Mark Rebholz at the controls. Mark Rebholz was keen to use the same navigation techniques used by Brown in 1919. Their experiences on the flight would have been familiar to Alcock and Brown: poor weather, communications

In 2005 the Vimy flew the Atlantic in the 'footsteps' of Alcock and Brown. (Leading Edge)

Sean Lemas speaking at the inauguration of the memorial commemorating their Ireland landing. (BAE Systems)

This cairn marks the site of Marconi's first transatlantic wireless station from where the aviators transmitted the news of their success. It is 500 metres from their actual landing site and 4 kilometres south of Clifden, Ireland. (Smb 1001)

This sculpture of an aircraft's tail-fin is on Errislannan Hill two kilometres north Connemara of their landing spot, dedicated on the fortieth anniversary of their landing, 15 June 1959. (Smb1001)

146

This statue to Alcock and Brown is in front of the Heathrow Academy, the former Visitor Centre, Heathrow. The inscription at the base says 'Sir John Alcock and Sir Arthur Whitten Brown who made the first direct flight across the Atlantic. St John's Newfoundland – Clifden Ireland 14th - 15th June 1919.' (Adrian Pingstone)

malfunctioning, the need to keep focussed on the task at all times with no time to rest, cold, fear of icing on the Vimy's surfaces, Mark even had to pass scribbled notes to Steve as his headset was dead. It was as if Alcock and Brown were somehow making sure that the re-enactment was as authentic as it could be. The major difference however was the landing. This time, Clifden was expecting the two aviators. There was to be no ignominious crash landing in a bog. Instead, a large crowd had gathered to greet them on a nearby golf course. This Vimy had flown the Atlantic, London to Australia and London to Cape Town, quite an accomplishment for a biplane designed in the First World War just sixteen years after Wilbur and Orville Wright made the first controlled, sustained, heavier-than-air flight. They flew about the length of a jumbo jet, the Vimy traversed the globe.

FIFTY YEARS LATER

1919 was a 'Golden Year' in the story of flight. It was a year of progress and achievement of global significance that touched the lives of millions around the world beyond the world of aviation. Fifty years later, two events were to dominate the world's headlines: the maiden flight of Concorde, the world's first supersonic airliner, and the successful Apollo 11 mission to put a man on the moon. Both events had a profound impact about how we see our world.

Almost lost in the excitement was a transatlantic race to commemorate the 50th anniversary of Alcock and Brown's Atlantic flight. Once again, the race was sponsored by the *Daily Mail* but the challenge was to set the fastest time between the top of London's Post Office Tower and the Empire State Building in New York.

There were twenty-one prizes across different categories and the race was run between 4 and 11 May 1969. The race was open to anyone, from pilots of Service aircraft to members of the public using charter or normal airline facilities.

Initially it was hoped that this would be an international competition and the United States Air Force considered entering a hypersonic B58 Hustler. However, with the ongoing conflict in Vietnam, the commitment of military resources for such a publicity-orientated display was politically inadvisable and as a result it was withdrawn.

The first civilian to start was Anne Alcock, niece of Sir John Alcock. She carried with her a package for Bob Tinker, Building Manager of the

Empire State Building. Anne had been specially appointed as a licenced mail carrier by the post office so that she could deliver a block of 50th anniversary Alcock and Brown stamps. These were to be sent on to the Postmaster General, just as Alcock and Brown had delivered their package of letters from Newfoundland as soon as they arrived in London fifty years earlier.

On the British side the Royal Navy entered three McDonnell Douglas FG.1 Phantoms which were to take off from the Floyd Bennet Naval Air Station south east of Brooklyn, New York, to Wisley aerodrome in Surrey. Using Wisley as the landing airfield was perhaps symbolic as this was the aerodrome formerly used by Vickers to test its aircraft. The Phantoms were refuelled over Newfoundland before making their supersonic dash across the Atlantic where they were then refuelled for the final leg back to Wisley. The first flight, made on 4 May, beat the existing transatlantic world speed record by 26 minutes having done it in 5½ hours. In his enthusiasm to save as much time as possible, pilot Lieutenant Commander Doug Borrowman burst two tyres on landing at Wisley bringing the Phantom to a speedy halt. On 11 May the third of the Royal Navy Phantoms of 892 Naval Air Squadron set a new world air speed record between New York and London of four hours and forty-six minutes.

The Royal Air Force decided to take a different tack and entered two Hawker Siddeley Harriers with the aim of flying both east to west and back. The advantage was that if the right take-off and landing sites could be found, they could operate much nearer the two iconic towers. But it seemed a risky decision as the Harrier was still being evaluated at Boscombe Down and was not yet in service.

Graham Williams was an RAF test pilot at Boscombe Down working on the Harrier programme when word came down that the RAF were going to enter two aircraft:

> GW: The first we heard of it was only two or three months before the event. Some bright spark in the Ministry of Defence came up with this idea of putting the Harrier into the Transatlantic Air Race. At the time we only had three pilots qualified – current – on the aeroplane. One was a guy called Mike Adams who was at Dunsfold as the Operational Requirements Liaison Officer (ORLO) and he had been at Boscombe before and he had been the Harrier project pilot and he had a hundred plus hours on the aeroplane. Tom Lecky-Thomson was the second

149

one and he had been flying it as the current project pilot at Boscombe and the only other pilot on the squadron who had flown it was me. I had only done about fifteen or twenty hours at the most. When they came up with this idea Mike Adams was the prime pilot with Tom Lecky-Thomson as the second pilot and I was nominated as a reserve just in case anything happened to anybody. I never thought it would come to pass, I thought the whole idea was crazy, to be honest. You don't take, in my view, an aeroplane which is a prototype, unproven in terms of reliability. At that stage of its life, it hadn't even entered service so you don't just take an aircraft and carry out some exercise like landing in the middle of New York and landing in the centre of London. Crazy!

Mike Adams was badly injured when the front wheel collapsed on the Harrier he was testing.

GW: I felt what was even more crazy was that when Mike Adams did his back in I was now one of the pilots going to take part in the air race. I had said to Tom Lecky-Thomson that I thought this was crazy and if we get away with it we will be bloody lucky. We were lucky!

My main concern was the fact that it was very early in the development days. To give you an example, three months later the engines were failing with an alarming regularity. If we had anything like that happen in the middle of New York or London it would have been an absolute disaster, one way or another. I did think that the whole exercise was premature.

When we started the exercise, we still had to do the air to air refuelling trials. We had to do long range, long distance stuff – seven-hour flights to make sure the oil consumption was not too great, the oxygen consumption wasn't too great and all that. We did all that in the few weeks running up to the air race.

I remember going around the United Kingdom about three times in a Harrier, taking off at about nine o'clock and landing back at about five in the afternoon just to prove the aircraft.

Back then, the Harrier's endurance fitted with small tanks was around an hour and a half.

The aircraft were only adapted in a small way, they had the wing tip extensions added which were said to extend the range of the aircraft. I think they did, a bit. I think that was the only time the wing tip extensions were ever used on the aircraft. When it went into service, they were too much trouble to bolt on and they did not extend enough range to be worthwhile.

I hadn't done air to air refuelling before and I remember when I was tasked with doing some air to air refuelling in the Harrier I said that this is all very well but I've never done air to air refuelling. So I went around trying to find an aeroplane to practise some air to air refuelling before I did it in the Harrier so that I had something to compare it against. In the end we didn't seem to have anything serviceable.

I rang up the Navy at Boscombe and asked if they had anything with a probe on it. They said they had a Scimitar sitting outside with a probe on it. I explained what I wanted to do and they said to pop down and that they would set it all up for me. I said that I had not flown the Scimitar before, and they said not to worry about that. So, I went down there and an hour later I was airborne in the Scimitar. They had arranged a Sea Vixen tanker from Yeovilton and there I was doing air to air refuelling in a Scimitar which was fortunate in that the layout is very similar in that the probe is on the nose, so it was not dissimilar to a Harrier. It turned out that the Scimitar was easy to refuel, and the Harrier was equally easy to refuel, not like a Lightning which was tricky because the probe was way back on the wing.

As far as preparing for any hazards – I made sure I had a decent immersion suit. Not only were we stretching a point for the aeroplane, we were flying at its maximum continuous setting for a whole five or six hours of the flight – Mach point eight-eight – so it was pushing things a bit. I had given vague thought to what I was going to do in a dinghy in the middle of the Atlantic but other than that, nothing special.

We were going to go up the east coast of the United States and Canada and head out over Newfoundland and then cross over Ireland and straight into London.

I was never going to win it from my side because the Navy had the Phantoms which were supersonic. To me, winning it was not so important as being seen to complete it in a vertical take-off in the middle of a city, and a vertical landing in the middle of another city having crossed the Atlantic. That was the thing and that as far as I was concerned, the achievement, winning was almost secondary.

I wasn't involved in the search for a landing place. Tom and Mike Adams went off to America to look for sites and we ended up with the jetty in the East River off Manhattan which was ideal. By the time I was tasked with the thing we were still looking for a landing place in London. For some reason that I never understood we were not allowed to land in one of the parks. Regents Park would have been the ideal place, but they would not let us land in the parks, so we had to look for another site.

Just before I left to go to the States (I went to the States two to three weeks before the event), they found this site at St Pancras. I had a quick look at it from the ground and that was the only time I looked at it but it looked alright to me and it was, it was ideal.

The start/finish line in New York was on the eighty-sixth floor of the Empire State Building. From there, Graham Williams had to get to a take-off pad.

GW: From the Empire State to the jetty in the East River is about fifteen minutes as I recollect, by car. When I arrived in New York, Jaguar gave me an E-Type, would you believe. I took one look at it and said, 'Excuse me, but I'm not going to drive that. I'll kill myself or get done by the police or something,' and so they gave me a little Austin America which was the old Austin 1100. But I still used the E-Type and had a guy drive me from the Empire State Building to the aircraft. That was a mistake. If I had used a motorbike, I would have been much quicker because I got terrible traffic. That was one of the reasons why I didn't do so well as I might have done.

The Americans were terribly helpful to us, they bent over backwards to help us, in fact I was surprised they were so cooperative, and the air traffic people were cooperative, and they bent over backwards to bend their rules for us. They were very good. It was about the time that the Marine Corps were buying the Harrier and John Farley and Mike went and displayed a couple of aircraft after the air race. But it was the Marines who laid the landing pad in the East River and gave us all the support in the world, and I am sure the Harrier's performance in the air race played its part in cementing the deal.

We were sat in a pub in New York and the news was on and there was this item on about the QE2 having its maiden voyage. We decided that we were not going to be outdone by them, we'll do something about that. So, we decided that we would greet the QE2 as it came up the Verrazano Narrows by hovering either side of the Bridge. At the time I thought if I should ask permission to do this but then I decided that no, it's much easier to beg for forgiveness after the event because if you ask for permission someone is always going to say no. So, we did it. As the QE2 came into New York she had two Harriers hovering either side of the bridge.

Having done that, we waited another twenty-four hours because the weather was terrible. It was a Friday and the air race finished on the Saturday so we could not afford to wait any longer, so we decided to go. The weather was so bad that JFK, the New York airport, was closed and that had to be bad weather even for those days.

Bill Bedford had been the chief test pilot at Hawkers who along with Hugh Merewether who pioneered the development of the Harrier was in New York as part of Hawker's support team. Bill was on the jetty and engaged the man from the FAA to keep him out of the way as the FAA guy wanted to stop me from going because of the weather. He started chatting to him in the tent. Meanwhile I was starting the engine up and before he realised what was going on I was airborne and that was thanks to Bill Bedford.

It was torrential rain although the cloud base had lifted just high enough to allow me to take off and transition into the cloud which was solid from about two hundred feet to thirty-six thousand. I went straight through the New York-Kennedy stack, but the controllers were absolutely wonderful to me. They wanted me to do a procedural turn, but I said I couldn't do it as the artificial horizon had toppled and I was a bit limited on instruments anyway. Tom's aeroplane had the full inertial system in it, mine only had the basic instruments in it, a hotchpotch of conventional flight instruments and it did not have any inertial system in it.

I went up through 36,000 feet of cloud, came out at the top and thought where are the tankers? because we did not have a lot of fuel on board and we didn't have a diversion because the whole of the East Coast was fogged out all the way up to Newfoundland. I hadn't realised quite how bad it was, so it was a case of find the tankers or else. Fortunately, as was always the case, the tankers were right there, on time, in the right place and I just caught a glimpse of them as I came out of the top of the cloud, trailing in the cloud tops so I was able to join up with them and refuel. I was low on fuel as I had to do a vertical take-off you can only have a certain weight and that amounted to 1800-2000 pounds of fuel which really is not a lot because you need to land. So you need to keep about 400 aside, 800 most. The climb took six, seven hundred pounds of fuel so there was not a lot of leeway.

The logistics plan was enormous. I think it took six tankers to get me across the Atlantic and the same for Tom the other way of course. Three tankers met me overhead New York and took me all the way up to Newfoundland. Three other tankers then moved in and the three tankers that were with me refuelled off them. The refuelling tankers peeled off and left the original three with me across the Atlantic. One of them went unserviceable and left us so I was left with two tankers. I had to refuel five or six times. You could probably do it with three refuellings but when you get to the middle of the Atlantic you always have to have enough fuel to divert if you can possibly do it. So, when you get to that middle bit of the Atlantic you have to keep topping up to make sure you have the range to meet the diversion. I was never convinced we were going to make it if we had to divert but we never did.

It was six refuellings but I declined the last one as I was up to the gunwales with fuel and then I had to start thinking about getting the fuel down to a level so that I could do a vertical landing at St Pancras.

As far as my arrival over England was concerned, there always has to be a bit of luck involved in these things. I dread to think what would have happened if the weather had been the same as it had been in New York. God knows where I would have ended up. But when I actually came across and hit Ireland (when I declined the refuelling), I hit about five hundred and fifty knots coming down in a dive.

I planned to hit 'Ally Pally' [Alexandra Palace, London], turn right to come down the railway to St Pancras. That seemed to be the easy way to do it and that's what I did. But there had just been a thunderstorm earlier that afternoon and this was about five o'clock in the evening. The visibility was something you never see over London in a month of Sundays. You could see from one side of London to the other. Because the thunderstorm had settled all the dust and everything else, it was wonderful. So, I had no trouble. I picked up Alexandra Palace from miles out. Aimed for that, turned right, straight down the railway line doing five hundred and fifty knots. I was so intrigued by the whole

For the 50th Anniversary the RAF entered 2 Harriers. It was an enormous risk as the Harrier had still not entered RAF service. (The Aviation Historian)

thing, I could even see the GPO Tower! I was quite excited by it! So much so that I nearly forgot to slow down. Anyhow, I did the fastest de-accelerating transition into the hover that I think I have ever done in my life, not by design, I'm afraid to say.

Tom took off in the same coal yard and it was dry when he took off and coal dust went everywhere. When I climbed into his aeroplane in New York I thought what has he been doing? Everything was black, there was coal dust everywhere in the cockpit. I had white gloves on and they were black in no time. But because there had been a thunderstorm it had settled all the coal dust and I did not have any trouble with it at all. So, I was lucky on two counts, first the weather was fine and also the thunderstorm had settled all the dust.

I was then put on the back of a motorbike who took me about a hundred yards and dumped me into this helicopter. I thought what the hell is going on here? I had no idea there was a little site outside the GPO Tower and so when I was shovelled out of the helicopter, I had no idea where I was but after a moment I realised and that was it.

RAF Harrier demonstrates its vertical take off from a coal yard by St Pancras station in London at the start of its flight to New York commemorating the 50th anniversary of Alcock & Brown's flight. (*The Aviation Historian*)

Right: The 50th Anniversary race was from the Post Office Tower in London to the top of the Empire State building in New York. Sqn Ldr Tom Lecky-Thompson was given a lift for the final stage in New York by a helpful off-duty policeman. (*The Aviation Historian*)

Below: The Harrier waiting on the improvised pad in downtown Manhattan for Graham Williams who was due to fly the return leg. (*The Aviation Historian*)

Originally, I thought that the whole exercise was madness and extremely risky; I remember saying to Tom beforehand that if we both got away with it, we would be very lucky. If it had gone wrong, it would have finished the Harrier programme.

I don't think what we went through was anything compared with what they [Alcock and Brown] went through. That first crossing of the Atlantic was an outstanding achievement in one way or the other. I think ours was pretty ordinary when compared.

1979 RAF CONINGSBY

In the late 1970s Squadron Leader Tony Alcock, nephew of Sir John Alcock, was a flight commander on No 56 Squadron at RAF Coningsby. They were now operating the McDonnell Douglas F4 Phantom. He managed to persuade the Air Force hierarchy that it would be a good idea to commemorate the 60th Anniversary of Alcock and Brown's flight with one of their own. Having got the necessary approval an aircraft was beautifully prepared. But Alcock wanted a suitably named navigator. This turned out

RAF Phantom flown by pilot Sqn Ldr AJN 'Tony' Alcock, nephew of Sir John and navigator Flt Lt Norman Browne to mark the 60th Anniversary. (A Flying History)

Rear view of the Phantom painted in a special scheme for the 60th anniversary flight. (A Flying History)

to be easier than expected, although a slight compromise had to be made on the spelling. Flight Lieutenant Norman Browne, a Buccaneer navigator, had also flown on Phantoms and was willing to join Tony for the trip. The aircraft also carried a special livery to commemorate the 30th Anniversary of NATO with members' badges added down the spine.

They left St Athan on 19 June and flew to Goose Bay, Newfoundland, from where the crossing was to be made. With them was 'Twinkletoe', one of the original black cat mascots carried in the Vimy. On 21 June they took off from Goose Bay and headed out over the Atlantic for Ireland. They flew subsonically but still set a new record of five hours and forty minutes. They had to be refuelled five times by Handley Page Victors. The Phantom is now preserved at the RAF Museum, Hendon.

APPENDICES

Mail Flights

The opportunity of using aircraft to transport mail and documents around the world was of huge importance in the development of air routes. Alcock and Brown's achievement meant that mail and packages could be transported between the United States and Europe in a fraction of the time it took by sea. But first they had to prove it could be done, which is why the contenders for the Atlantic prize were asked to carry small bags of mail in their aircraft. It also provided some measure of proof that the aircraft had actually left Newfoundland.

The idea of carrying mail across the Atlantic in a matter of hours rather than the many days that the journey took by boat was clearly of interest to the Newfoundland Post Office. So on 5 April 1919 they wrote to the Sopwith Aviation Company:

> On what terms will you carry a small official mail, the number of items not to exceed ten, and the weight not to exceed one pound? As an alternative proposition, and subject to such limitations as may be agreed, upon on what terms will you carry a general letter mail?

Mr Fenn on behalf of Sopwith Aviation Company, replied on 8 April:

> My Company will be prepared to accept this on the two following conditions
>
> (1) That the Sopwith Aviation Co. Ltd. be allowed to carry a maximum of 100 letters in excess of the ten mentioned above.
> (2) That the Sopwith Aviation Co. Ltd. be paid the sum of one dollar, to be paid to them by cheque made payable to the Company.
>
> It is clearly understood that in the event of the Sopwith Aeroplane being subsidised by the Newfoundland Government, it must be the first to attempt of the crossing of the Atlantic by air.

Agreement was reached, but as all the aviators were essentially in a race to be the first across, the Newfoundland Post Office put a small sting in the tail:

It is, however, to be understood between us that should the Martinsyde or any other airship get away before the Sopwith machine, you agree on your part to promptly return the bag of mail to my order, so that it may be sent by the first airship to leave.

Two hundred examples of the current 3c brown Caribou stamp were hastily overprinted 'FIRST / TRANS- / ATLANTIC / AIR / POST / APRIL 1919'. Eighteen of these proved to be defective and were destroyed; ninety-five were used in letters carried by Hawker and his navigator, Mackenzie Grieve; eleven were presented to various officials, and the remaining 76 sold for $25 each in May 1919.

The Sopwith remained drifting on the sea until it was salvaged by the SS *Lake Charlottesville* on 23 May. In a telegraph to the Secretary of the Navy, Lieutenant Commander A.C. Wilvers reported:

> Near the top of the plane was lashed a brown postage bag which was marked 'Newfoundland G.P.O.' It contained mail mostly addressed to prominent British Peers, the Royal Family and one addressed to His Majesty the King. The mail was very soaked and otherwise damaged.

The *Lake Charlottesville* arrived at Falmouth on 28 May and the wrecked aircraft was handed over to the local customs and excise officials. The mail was sent to London and put into the British postal system on 30 May.

Although it was intended that the US Navy flight would carry an official commemorative mail, it was taken off to save weight and no official mail was carried, although one letter was flown unofficially.

Once again the Newfoundland Post Office decided to prepare a special stamp to mark the occasion. This time the current 3c. Caribou stamp was given a manuscript overprint reading 'Aerial / Atlantic / Mail / J.A.R. [the initials of J. Alex Robinson, the Postmaster General]'. We do not know precisely how many were given this overprint, but it probably amounted to less than fifty. After the crash on 17 July, Raynham returned to England by ship, taking the mail bag with him, but he forgot to hand it to the authorities. When, months later, enquiries were made about it, he remembered that it was with his luggage – which he had never unpacked, apparently! It was handed over on 7 January 1920, and received the London backstamp of that date. These are among the rarest air mail stamps in the world.

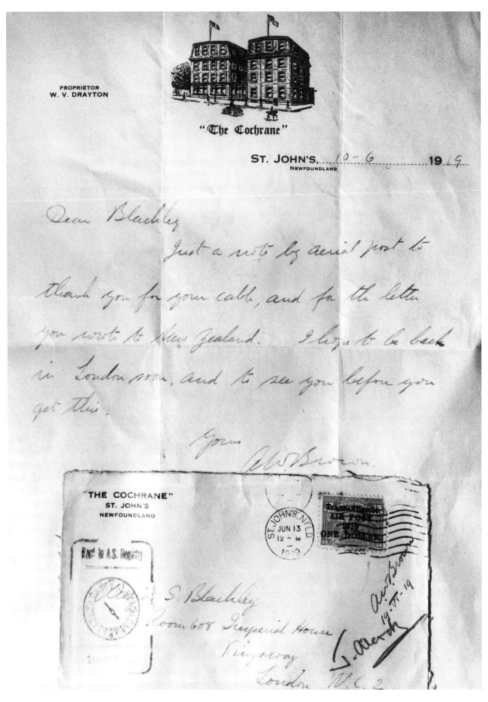

The first transatlantic airmail delivered by Alcock and Brown. (BAE Systems)

BUCKINGHAM PALACE

July 28th, 1919.

Dear Sir John Alcock,

      The King is, as you know, a great collector of stamps, and I am writing to ask whether you could possibly let me have for His Majesty's collection the envelope of one of the letters you brought over with you in your Atlantic Flight with one of the special Newfoundland stamps which is overprinted "transatlantic air post, 1919 $1" on the envelope.

      If you happen to have a spare one of these, I know that the King would greatly appreciate it if you were able to present it to His Majesty.

                Believe me,

                     Yours very truly,

Sir John Alcock,
        K.B.E.
           Air Ministry,
              Empire House, Kingsway.

The King who was an enthusiastic stamp collector wrote to Sir John Alcock requesting one of the specially franked stamps for the royal collection. (BAE Systems)

Undeterred by the two previous attempts, the Newfoundland Post Office once again made arrangements for mail to be carried on Alcock and Brown's flight, and also that of Admiral Kerr's four-engine Handley Page bomber which had recently arrived. In contrast to the severely limited numbers of special stamps prepared for the two earlier flights, 10,000 examples of the 1897 15c. were surcharged 'Trans-Atlantic/AIR POST/1919/ONE DOLLAR' with 50c. for each stamp sold being donated to the Permanent Marine Disasters Fund.

The rarity of the Hawker and Martinsyde issues was already apparent and this time the Post Office was going to make certain there were enough stamps to go round. The weight considerations of the earlier attempts were still very much a problem and Alcock and Brown's post consisted of just 196 letters and one letter packet.

Charges to Clear Lester's Field

By the time Alcock and Brown arrived in Newfoundland the best sites for an airfield had been taken by Harry Hawker at Mount Pearl, Freddy Raynham at Quidi Vidi, and Admiral Kerr at Harbour Grace. With mounting desperation Alcock travelled the country looking for a suitable ground. Although Raynham sportingly gave them the use of his field, Alcock was concerned that it was too short for a fully-laden Vimy to take off from. Very late in the day local farmer Charles F. Lester came to their rescue with the offer of a strip which, with 'modifications', Alcock thought they could use. The following is taken from the receipt for the charges to clear the land:

> 2079 Hours @ .40 per hour = $831.60
>
> 330 Hours extra @ .25 per hour = 82.50
>
> Pussages [sic] Allowance 30 men @ $1.20 = $36.00
>
> Horse Labour = $165.00
>
> Expenses for Securing Labour = $20.00
>
> Coal for Shack = $10.00
>
> Sub-Total: $1,145.10
>
> Commission on Work = $150.00
>
> Monday & Tuesdays Work on Field = $50.00
>
> Total: $1,345.10

Brown on Navigation

Although Brown was largely a self-taught navigator, he was not an amateur. He had read as much as he could and had used the time as they travelled out to Newfoundland on the *Mauretania* to get plenty of practice and refine his knowledge. He was adapting long-established maritime navigation techniques, some of which were hundreds if not thousands of years old to work in an aerial setting. The problem was that nobody had any real idea what happens at several thousand feet over the Atlantic because nobody had been there. As Oswald Short had pointed out before their ill-fated attempt from east to west, wind direction and strength changes at different altitudes. The RAF meteorologist Lieutenant Clements had given him as much information as he had gleaned from radio reports from ships out at sea, but there were gaps in the data. As things turned out, the weather was appalling, and Brown was unable to take the readings he needed with any degree of accuracy. But he doggedly monitored their speed and direction, making adjustments to their course as he felt necessary. What is remarkable is that they landed only thirty miles from where they had originally intended. Thus, as they took off from Lester's Field that June afternoon, they really were setting off on a flight into the unknown.

Sir Arthur Whitten Brown: The navigation of aircraft, in its present stage, is distinctly more difficult than the navigation of sea craft. The speed at which they travel, and the influence of the wind introduce problems which are not easily solved.

A ship's navigator knows to a small fraction of a mile the set of any ocean current, and from the known speed of his vessel he can keep 'dead reckoning' with an accuracy that is nearly absolute. In fact, navigators have taken their craft across the Atlantic without once having seen the sun or stars, and yet, at the end of the journey, been within five miles of the desired destination. But in the air the currents either cannot be, or have not yet been, charted, and this allowance for the drift resulting from them must be obtained by direct observation on the surface of the ocean.

By the same means his actual speed over the ocean may be calculated. He finds the position of his craft by measuring the angle which either the sun or a selected star makes with the horizon, and noting the Greenwich mean time at which the observation is made. If the bearings of two distinct wireless stations can be taken, it is also possible to find his definite position by means of directional wireless telegraphy.

When making my plans for the transatlantic flight I considered very carefully all the possibilities and decided to rely solely upon observations of the sun and stars and upon 'dead reckoning', in preference to using directional wireless, as I was uncertain at that time whether or not the directional wireless system was sufficiently reliable.

My sextant was of the ordinary marine type, but it had a more heavily engraved scale than is usual, so as to make easier the reading of it amid the vibration of the aeroplane. My main chart was on the Mercator projection, and I had a special transparent chart which could be moved above it, and upon which were drawn the Sumner circles for all times of the day. I carried a similar special chart for use at night, giving the Sumner circles for six chosen stars. To measure the drift, I had a six-inch Drift-Bearing plate, which also permitted me to measure the ground speed, with the help of a stopwatch. In addition, I had an Appleyard Course and Distance Calculator, and Traverse tables for the calculation of 'dead reckoning'.

As the horizon is often obscured by clouds or mist, making impossible the measurement of its angle with the heavenly bodies, I had a special type of spirit level, on which the horizon was replaced by a bubble. This, of course, was less reliable than a true horizon since the bubble was affected by variations of speed; but it was at least a safeguard. Taking into account the general obscurity of the atmosphere during most of the flight, it was fortunate that I took such a precaution, for I seldom caught sight of a clearly defined horizon.

Brown on the Future of Transatlantic Flight

As Brown said, this was the first generation of mankind 'to see flying dreams and theories translated into fact'. He foresaw a future when aviation could create the possibility of a peaceful, prosperous world, where flight would knit the world together, not become the latest weapon.

RACE ACROSS THE ATLANTIC

Although three pioneer flights were made across the Atlantic during the summer of 1919, the year passed, as did the next, without bringing to light any immediate prospect of an air service between Europe and America:

> Before a transatlantic airway is possible, much remains to be done–organization, capitalization, government support, the charting of air currents, the establishment of directional wireless stations, research after improvements in the available material. All this requires the spending of money; and for the moment neither governments nor private interests are enamoured of investments with a large element of speculation.
>
> But, sooner or later, a London–New York service of aircraft must be established. Its advantages are too tremendous to be ignored for long. Prediction is ever dangerous; and, meantime, I am confining myself to a discussion of what can be done with the means and the knowledge already at the disposal of experts, provided their brains are allied to sufficient capital.
>
> Notwithstanding that the first two flights across the Atlantic were made respectively by a flying-boat and an aeroplane, it is very evident that the future of transatlantic flight belongs to the airship. That the apparatus in which Sir John Alcock and I made the first non-stop air journey over the Atlantic was an aeroplane only emphasizes my belief that for long flights above the ocean the dirigible is the only useful vehicle. If science discovers some startlingly new motive power–for example, intermolecular energy–that will revolutionize mechanical propulsion, heavier-than-air craft may be as valuable for long flights as for air traffic over shorter distances. Until then trans-ocean flying on a commercial basis must be monopolized by lighter-than-air craft.
>
> The aeroplane–and in this general term I include the flying boat and the seaplane–is impracticable as a means of transport for distances over one thousand miles, because it has definite and scientific limitations of size, and consequently of lift. The ratio of weight to power would prevent a forty-ton aeroplane– which is approximately the largest heavier-than-air craft that at present might be constructed and effectively handled–from remaining aloft in still air for longer than twenty-five hours, carrying a load of passengers and mails of about five tons at

an air speed of, say, eighty-five miles an hour. Its maximum air distance, without landing to replenish the fuel supply, would thus be two thousand, one hundred and twenty-five miles. For a flight of twenty-five hundred miles all the disposable lift (gross lift minus weight of structure) would be needed for crew and fuel, and neither passengers nor freight could be taken aboard.

There is not in existence an aeroplane capable of flying, without alighting on the way, the three thousand miles between London and New York, even when loaded only with the necessary crew. With the very smallest margin of safety no transatlantic route of over two thousand miles is admissible for aeroplanes. This limitation would necessitate time-losing and wearisome journeys between London and Ireland, Newfoundland and New York, to and from the nearest points on either side of the ocean. Even under these conditions only important mail or valuable articles of little weight might be carried profitably.

As against these drawbacks, the larger types of airships have a radius far wider than the Atlantic. Their only limit of size is concerned with landing grounds and sheds; for the percentage of useful lift increases with the bulk of the vessel, while the weight to power ratio decreases. A voyage by dirigible can therefore be made directly from London to New York, and far beyond it, without a halt. Another advantage of lighter-than-air craft is that whereas the restricted space on board an aeroplane leaves little for comfort and convenience, a large rigid airship can easily provide first-rate living, sleeping and dining quarters, besides room for the passengers to take exercise by walking along the length of the inside keel, or on the shelter deck. In a saloon at the top of the vessel no noise from the engines would be heard, as must be the case in whatever quarters could be provided on a passenger aeroplane.

Yet another point in favour of the airship as a medium for trans-ocean flight is its greater safety. An aeroplane is entirely dependent for sustentation in the air on the proper working of all its motors. Should two motors–in some cases even one– break down, the result would be a forced descent into the water, with the possibility of total loss on a rough sea, even though the craft be a solid flying boat. In the case of an airship the only result of the failure of any of the motors is reduction

168

of speed. Moreover, a speed of four-fifths of the maximum can still be maintained with half the motors of an airship out of action, so that there is no possibility of a forced descent owing to engine breakdown. The sole result of such a mishap would be to delay the vessel's arrival. Further, it may be noted that an airship's machinery can be so arranged as to be readily accessible for repairs and replacement while on a voyage.

As regards comparative speed the heavy type of aeroplane necessary to carry an economical load for long distances would not be capable of much more than eighty-five to ninety miles an hour. The difference between this and the present airship speed of sixty miles an hour would be reduced by the fact that an aeroplane must land at intermediate stations for fuel replenishment. Any slight advantage in speed that such heavier-than-air craft possess will disappear with the future production of larger types of dirigible, capable of cruising speeds varying from seventy-five to ninety miles an hour. For the airship service London–New York direct, the approximate time under normal conditions should be fifty hours. For the aeroplane service London–Ireland–Newfoundland–New York the time would be at least forty-six hours.

Perhaps the most convincing argument in favour of airships as against aeroplanes for trans-ocean aviation is that of comparative cost. All air estimates under present conditions must be very approximate; but I put faith in the carefully prepared calculations of experts of my acquaintance. These go to show that, with the equipment likely to be available during the next few years, a regular and effective air service between London and New York will need (again emphasizing the factor of approximation) the following capital and rates:

	Airship Service [1]	Aeroplane Service [2]
Capital required	$13,000,000	$19,300,000
Passenger rate:		
London–New York	$240	$575
Rate per passenger:		
Mile	8 cents	18 cents
Mails per ounce:		
London–New York	6¼ cents	15½ cents

These figures for an airship service are based on detailed calculations, of which the more important are:

Capital Charges:

Four airships of 3,500,000 cu. ft. capacity, at $2,000,000 each	$8,000,000
Two double airship sheds at $1,500,000 each	3,000,000
Land for two sheds and aerodromes at $150,000 each	300,000
Workshops, gas plants, and equipment	750,000
Working capital, including spare parts, stores, etc.	850,000
Wireless equipment	50,000
Miscellaneous accessories	50,000
Total capital required	$13,000,000
Annual charge, interest at 10%	$1,300,000

Depreciation and Insurance:
Airships.
Useful life, about 3 years.
Obsolete value, about $100,000 per ship.
Total depreciation per ship, $1,900,000 in three years.
Average total depreciation per annum for four ships for 3 years, $2,535,000.

Airship sheds.	
Total annual charge	$90,000
Workshops and plant.	
Depreciation at 5% per annum	17,500
Total annual charge for depreciation	2,650,000
Total annual insurance charges on airships and plant	617,500

Annual Establishment Expenses:
Salaries of Officers and Crews–4 airship
  commanders; 8 airship officers; 54 Crew hands $130,000

Salaries of Establishment–Management and Staff; Workshop hands, storekeepers, etc. (50 at each shed–total 100)	$125,000
Total annual establishment expenses	$255,000
Repairs and Maintenance:	
Sheds and plant, annual charge, say,	$25,000
Repairs and overhaul of airships	100,000
Total charge	$125,000
Total annual charges on above basis	$4,947,500
Say	$5,000,000
Cost Chargeable per Crossing:	
Taking the total number of crossings per year as 200 (London-New York)–Proportion of annual charges per crossing	$25,000
Petrol per trip, 30 tons at $125 per ton.	3,750
Oil per trip, 2 tons at $200 per ton	400
Hydrogen used, 750,000 cu. ft. at $2.50 per 1,000 cu. ft.	1,875
Cost of food per trip for crew of 19 and 100 passengers	2,000
Total charge per crossing (London-New York)	$33,025

The weight available for passengers and mails on each airship of the type projected would be fifteen tons. This permits the carrying of one hundred and forty passengers and effects, or ten tons of mails and fifty passengers. To cover the working costs and interest, passengers would have to be charged $240 per head and mails $2,025 per ton for the voyage London–New York.

This charge for passengers is already less than that for the more expensive berths on transatlantic liners. Without a doubt, with the coming of cheaper fuel, lower insurance rates and larger airships, it will be reduced eventually to the cheapest rate for first-class passages on sea liners.

With a fleet of four airships, a service of two trips each way per week is easily possible. For aeroplanes with a total load of forty tons the weight available for passengers and mails is 2.1 tons. If such a craft were to carry the same weekly load as the service of airships—thirty tons each way—it would be necessary to have fourteen machines continually in commission. Allowing for one hundred per cent. spare craft as standby for repairs and overhaul, twenty-eight aeroplanes would be required. The approximate cost of such a service is:

Capital Charges:	
28 aeroplanes at $600,000 each	$16,750,000
28 aeroplane sheds at $50,000 each	1,400,000
Land for 4 aerodromes	500,000
Workshops and equipments	100,000
Spare parts, etc.	500,000
Wireless equipment	50,000
Total capital required	$19,300,000
Annual charge at 10% interest	$1,930,000

Depreciation and Insurance:	
Aeroplanes.	
Useful life, say 3 years, as for airships.	
Obsolete value, say, $30,000 per machine.	
Average total depreciation per annum for 28 machines	$5,250,000
Aeroplane Sheds.	
Total annual charge	60,000
Workshops and Plant.	
Depreciation at 3% per annum	3,000
Total annual charge for depreciation	5,314,000
Total annual insurance charges on machinery and plant	1,152,000

Annual Establishment Expenses:	
Salaries of 36 pilots at $3,000 per annum	$108,000
Salaries of 36 engineers at $2,000 per annum	72,000
Salaries of 12 stewards at $1,500 per annum	18,000
Salaries of establishment–	
Management and staff	25,000
Workshop hands and storekeepers, etc., 100 off	100,000
Total annual establishment expcnses	$323,000

Repairs and Maintenance:

Sheds and plant, annual charge, say	$25,000
Repairs and overhaul to machines	50,000
Total.	$75,000
Total annual charges on above basis	$8,792,500

Cost chargeable per crossing:

Proportion of annual charges per crossing	$7,250
Petrol used per trip, 28 tons at $125 per ton	3,500
Oil per trip, 2 tons at $200 per ton	400
Cost of food per trip for 29 passengers and crew of seven	500
	$11,650

It will be seen from the above that the direct running cost is 38%, and the overhead charges 62% of the total cost.

With a weight of 2.1 tons available on each machine for passengers and mails twenty passengers might be carried. To cover the working costs and interest they must be charged $575 per head. The rate for mails would be $5,500 per ton.

Having made clear that the airship is the only means of transatlantic flight on a paying basis, the next point to be considered is the type of dirigible necessary. A discussion at present of the size of the airships that will link Europe and America can be little more substantial than guesswork. The British dirigible R-34, which last year made the famous pioneer voyage between England and the United States, is too small for commercial purposes, with its disposable lift of twenty-nine tons and its gas capacity of less than two million cubic feet. Experts have predicted the use of airships of five million and ten million cubic feet capacity, with respective weights of thirty tons and one hundred tons available for passengers and freight.

It is probable, however, that such colossi must await birth for many years, and that a beginning will be made with moderate-sized craft of about three million, five hundred thousand cubic feet capacity, similar to those that serve as the basis of the estimates for a service between London and New York. A combination of British interests is planning to send ships of this type all over the world. These can be built immediately, and there are already in existence suitable sheds to house them. Details of their structure and capabilities may be of interest.

The projected airship of three million, five hundred thousand cubic feet capacity is capable of carrying a useful load of fifteen tons (passengers and mails) for a distance of forty-eight hundred miles in eighty hours, at the normal cruising speed. The total lifting power is one hundred and five tons, and the disposable lift (available for fuel, oil, stores, crew, passengers and freight) is sixty-eight tons. The maximum engine power is thirty-five hundred h. p., the maximum speed seventy-five miles an hour. The normal flying speed, using a cruising power of two thousand h. p., is sixty miles an hour. The overall length is eight hundred feet, the maximum diameter and width one hundred feet, and the overall height one hundred and five feet. These particulars and performances are based on present design, and on the results attained with ships of two million cubic feet capacity, now in service. The figures are conservative, and it is probable that a disposable lift greater than that of the specifications will be obtained as a result of improved structural efficiency.

The passenger accommodation will be such that the air journey can be made in comfort equal to that on a first-class liner of the sea. Apart from their comparatively small disposable lift, a main objection to vessels of the R-34 type for commercial purposes is that the living quarters are in cars slung from under the middle envelope. In this position they are necessarily rather cramped. In the proposed craft of three million, five hundred thousand cubic feet capacity the passengers' quarters are at the top of the vessel. There, they will be roomy and entirely free from the vibration of the engines. They are reached through an internal corridor across the length of the ship, or by elevator, from the bottom of it.

The main room is a large saloon lounge fitted with tables and chairs in the style of a Pullman car. Around it are windows, allowing for daylight and for an outlook in every direction. Part of it is fire-proofed and serves as a smoking room.

Next to, and communicating with, the lounge is the dining saloon. This leads to a serving hatch and electrical cooking apparatus. Electrical power is provided by dynamos driven off the main engines. Current for electric lighting and heating of the saloons, cars and sleeping quarters is provided by the same method.

Sleeping accommodation is in four-berth and two-berth cabins on top of the airship and forward of the living saloons. The cabins are of the type and size fitted on ocean-going steamers. With them are the usual bathrooms and offices. Other conveniences are an open shelter deck at the vessel's aft end, to enable passengers to take the air, and an observation car, fitted below the hull and also at the aft end, so that they can observe the land or sea directly below them.

No danger from fire need be feared. The machinery installation is carefully insulated from the gas bags, and the quarters are to be rendered fire-proof and gas-proof. Moreover, the amount of weight involved by the passengers' section is so small, compared with the weight of the machinery, fuel, cargo and stores, carried in the lower part of the craft, that the stability of the ship for rolling is unaffected by the novel position of the living quarters.

The ship's officers will have on the hull, towards the forward end, a control and navigation compartment, containing the main controls, navigation instruments, charts, and a cabin for the wireless telegraphy installation. The windows of this car give a clear view in every direction.

Other general specifications are:

Hull Structure. The shape of the hull is of the most perfect streamline form within the limitations of constructional requirements. An internal keel corridor, running along the bottom of the hull, contains all petrol and oil tanks and the water ballast.

Outer Covering. The outer cover is made of special weather-proof fabric, which gives the longest possible life. This fabric is as efficient as possible in insulating the gas from change of temperature, and thus avoids great variations in the lift.

Gasbags. The gas capacity is divided up into gasbags made of suitable rubber-proofed cotton fabric, lined with gold-beaters' skins. Gasbags will be fitted to automatic relief valves and hand control manoeuvring valves.

Machinery Cars. Six machinery cars are provided, each containing one engine installation, with a direct-driven propeller fitted at the aft end. These compartments give the mechanics easy access to each of the six engines and allow them to handle all parts of the machinery. Engine room telegraphs of the electrical type communicate between the forward compartment and each of the machinery cars.

Whereas the living quarters and the control compartment must be heated by electric radiators, arrangements can be made to warm the machinery cars by using the exhaust heat. The transmission gear in two of the wing cars is to be fitted with reversing gear, so that the craft may be driven astern. So that passengers shall not be worried by the usual roar of the exhaust, special silencers will be fitted. The transmission gear is also so arranged that all unnecessary clamour from it may be avoided.

The engines run on gasoline fuel, but they have devices whereby they can be run alternatively on hydrogen gas. They are designed to develop their maximum power at a height of five thousand feet.

Telephones. Telephone communication links all stations on the airship.

Landing Gear. Inflated buffer landing bags of a special type are to be fitted underneath the Forward Control Compartment and underneath the two Aft Machinery Cars. These enable the airship to alight either on land or on the sea's surface.

Wireless Telegraphy. A powerful wireless telegraphy installation is to be fitted in the wireless cabin in the forward control compartment. It will have a range for sending and receiving of at least five thousand miles.

Crew. Two watches would be required, taking duty in eight-hour shifts. Both must be on duty when the craft leaves or lands. Each watch consists of navigating officer, steersman, elevator man, four engineers and a wireless operator. With the commanding officer and two stewards, whose duties are not regulated by watches, the crew thus numbers nineteen men.

Although the speed of the airship at maximum power is seventy miles per hour, the crossing normally would be made at sixty miles per hour, which only requires two thousand horse power, and is much more economical in fuel. The full speed, however, can be used whenever the ship is obliged to voyage through storm areas or against strong head winds. By the Azores route, the time needed for the journey of thirty-six hundred miles, at a speed of sixty miles per hour, is sixty hours; but to allow for delays owing to adverse weather, the airship would always carry eighty hours' fuel, allowing for a speed of sixty miles per hour. The normal time for the journey from London to New York, via Portugal and the Azores (thirty-six hundred miles) would be, therefore, two-and-one-half days. The normal time for the journey New York to London by the direct route (three thousand miles) would be just over two days.

The prevailing wind on the direct route is almost always from West to East, which favours the Eastbound journey, but is unfavourable to the Westbound journey. It is proposed that the crossing Eastward from New York to London be made by the most direct route, advantage thus being taken of the Westerly winds.

By making the Westbound journey on the Southerly route, via the Coast of Portugal and the Azores, and on 35′ N. parallel of latitude across the Atlantic, and then to New York, the voyage is made in a region where the prevailing Westerly winds of the higher latitudes are absent, and only light winds are encountered, generally of a favourable direction. This route, however, adds about six hundred miles to the distance. With a ship speed of sixty miles per hour, it would be quicker to make the Westbound journey by the direct route if the Westerly wind did not exceed ten miles per hour. If the wind were greater, time would be saved by covering the extra six hundred miles of the Southerly route and dodging the unfavourable air currents.

With four airships on the Cross-Atlantic airway, two only would be in service at a time, so that each could lay up during alternate weeks for overhaul and refit. As the time of journey between London and New York will vary between fifty to sixty hours, each airship can easily make two crossings or one double journey per week, thus giving a service, with two dirigibles, of two 'sailings' each way per week.

The average time table might therefore be as follows:

LEAVE LONDON	ARRIVE NEW YORK
Monday morning	Wednesday afternoon or evening
Thursday morning	Saturday afternoon or evening

LEAVE NEW YORK	ARRIVE LONDON
Monday afternoon	Thursday morning
Thursday afternoon	Sunday morning.

From available weather reports, it is considered that crossings are practicable on at least three hundred days in the year. Probably a total of two hundred crossings in the year could be maintained. Until further study of weather conditions supplies a certain knowledge of the best possible altitudes and latitudes, it is likely that a regular service of two crossings each way per week will be maintained only in the months of May to September, and that the crossings from October to April will be irregular, the day of departure being dependent on the weather.

Weather difficulties are likely to be much less severe than might be imagined. Rain, hail and snow should have little influence on the navigation of airships. An outer covering that is rainproof and non-absorbent avoids the absorption of water and the consequent increase of weight. Hail and snow cannot adhere to the surface of the craft when in flight, owing to its high speed through the air; and, in any case, the precipitation height being not more than eight thousand feet, they can be avoided by flying above this altitude.

Fog may give trouble in landing, but during the journey an airship can keep above it. If the terminal were enveloped by fog an arriving ship could pass on to an emergency landing ground away from the fog-belt; if the mistiness were slight, it could remain in the air until the ground were visible, making use of its margin of fuel beyond the amount necessary for the London–New York flight. Airships in fog may be enabled to find their landing ground by means of captive balloons or kites, and of strong searchlights from the ground. At night, the balloons or kites could carry electric lights, with connections from the aerodrome.

In any case, fog, rain, hail and snow are nearly always local in their occurrence, and can be avoided by a short deviation from the usual route. Atlantic records indicate that on the main steamship routes fog sufficient to impede navigation does not occur on more than about twelve days in the year.

Wind is a factor that needs more careful study in its relation to transatlantic air navigation. In most cases, unduly strong winds can be dodged by flying on a higher level, or by cruising on a different course, so as to avoid the storm belt. Heavy storms, which are usually of a cyclonic nature, rarely cover an area of more than two hundred miles diameter. Moreover, the rate of progression of a cyclonic area is much less than the speed of the air movement. An airship is able to shake off a cyclonic area by a deviation from its course of not more than two hundred miles. Once away from the storm belt, it has no difficulty in keeping clear of it.

When higher levels of the air have been charted, there is every reason to believe that the known movements of the Atlantic winds will be used to shorten air journeys. There are at sea level, between certain clearly defined latitudes, prevailing winds of constant direction. At greater heights, also, there is in most latitudes a constant drift which, if charted, might be useful even if winds at sea level were unfavourable.

Although precise information is available of the prevailing and periodic winds at sea level in various latitudes, very little coordinated work appears to have been done in charting the prevailing and seasonal winds in higher levels of the atmosphere. Observations of the air currents over various localities in the United States, England and Germany have been taken, but very little is known of the winds above the great ocean tracts. There is a great necessity for international research to provide data for predictions of weather conditions in the upper atmosphere and thus enable advantage to be taken of these higher currents.

At high altitudes, constant winds of from thirty to forty miles per hour are common. If the prevailing directions of those were known to airship navigators, the duration of the journey could be considerably shortened, even if this meant taking an indirect route. It is undesirable to fly at great heights owing to the low temperature; but with suitable provision for heating there is no reason why flying at ten thousand feet should not be common.

Air currents cannot be charted as exactly as sea currents; but much valuable work can and will be done by tabulating in detail, for the guidance of air navigators, the tendencies of the Atlantic atmospheric drifts. Reliable charts, used in conjunction with directional messages from wireless stations and ships, may make it possible for vessels on the London–New York air service always to avoid troublesome winds, as well as storms and fogs, and to reduce the percentage of risk to a figure not exceeding that relative to sea liners.

For the rest, the excellence of the most modern engines and the fact that one or two, or even three of them can be temporarily out of action without affecting the airship's stability during a flight, minimize the danger of a breakdown from loss of power. The only remaining obstacle to reasonable safety would seem to be in landing on and departing from the terminal during rough weather. This can be overcome by the recently patented Vickers Mooring Gear for Rigid Airships.

The gear, designed so as to permit an airship to land and remain moored in the open for extended periods in any weather without the use of sheds, consists principally of a tall steel mast or tower, about one hundred and fifty feet in height, with a revolving head to which the craft is rigidly attached by the nose, permitting it to ride clear of the ground and to turn round in accordance with the direction of the wind. It is provided with a hauling-in winch and rope to bring the ship up to the mooring point.

An elevator, for passengers and goods, runs up the tower from the ground to the platform adjoining the nose of the airship. The passengers reach their quarters along a passage through the vessel, and the goods are taken down a runway. An airship moored to this mast can remain unharmed in even the worst weather, and need be taken into a shed only when overhaul and repairs are necessary.

RACE ACROSS THE ATLANTIC

In discussing the future of transatlantic flight, I have confined myself to the projected service between London and New York. There is likely to be another route over the Atlantic–London to Rio de Janeiro, via Lisbon and Sierra Leone. Already in London tickets are on sale at $5,000 apiece for the first flight from London to Rio. This, of course, is a freak price, which covers the distinction of being in the first airship to travel from England to Brazil. If and when a regular London–Rio service is established, the ordinary passenger rate should be little more than the $240 estimated as the air fare on the London–New York route.

It may be that the London–New York air service will not arrive for many years. Sooner or later, however, it must arrive; for science, allied to human enterprise, never neglects a big idea. It may be that, when it does arrive, the structure of the craft and the methods of navigation applied to them will differ in important details from what I have indicated. I make no pretence at prophecy, but have merely tried to show how, with the means already at hand, moderately priced air journeys from Europe to America can be made in two to two and a half days, with comfort, safety and a high degree of reliability. Meanwhile, much depends on the funds available for the erection of stations for directional wireless messages, on research into the air currents at various levels above the Atlantic Ocean, on the courage of capitalists in promoting what seems to be a very speculative enterprise, and on new adaptations of old mechanical inventions.

Already hundreds of aeroplanes, as time-saving vehicles, are used regularly in many countries for commercial traffic over comparatively short distances–the carriage of mails, passengers, valuable freight and urgent special journeys. When, but not until, the hundreds become thousands, and the longer distances are as well served by airships as are the shorter distances by aeroplanes, the world's air age will be in sight.

INDEX

Eastchurch, 11, 35, 52
Empire State Building, 148–9,
    152, 157

Far Rockaway, Long Island, 55

Gallipoli, 12

Halifax, Nova Scotia, 44, 52, 55, 59
Hanworth Air Park, 27
Harbour Grace, Newfoundland, 35,
    58, 86, 90, 164
Horta, 66

Kedos, 13

Lemnos, 11
Lester's Field, Newfoundland, 91–2,
    94–5, 164–5
Lisbon, Portugal, 46, 84, 181
London, 1–2, 8, 27–8, 43, 54, 76–7,
    85, 93, 101, 120, 124, 127,
    130–3, 136, 138, 141–3, 148–9,
    150–2, 155–7, 161, 167–9, 171,
    173, 177–8, 180–1

Manchester, 11, 13–15, 97, 130, 138
Manhattan, 6, 152, 157
Martlesham Heath, 38
Mount Pearl, Newfoundland, 48,
    56, 67–8, 88, 91, 104, 164

New York, 1, 6, 18, 54, 85, 127,
    140, 148–50, 152–4, 156–7,
    167–9, 171, 173, 177–8, 180–1

Paris, 2–3, 18, 85, 134, 136, 138
Placentia Bay, 47
Plymouth, England, 46, 84–5
Ponta Delgada, 63–5, 84
Post Office Tower, London,
    148, 157

Quidi Vidi, Newfoundland, 51, 53,
    57, 67, 69, 76, 79, 83, 86, 88,
    90, 140, 164

Rouen, France, 136, 138
Royal Aero Club, 3, 10–11, 17, 22,
    24, 50, 54, 77, 93, 124, 130–1
Rugby, 131

Savoy Hotel, 77, 132–3
Smyrna, 13
Somme, 15
St John's, Newfoundland, 19, 29,
    43, 46–51, 54, 56–9, 62, 66,
    69, 89, 91, 97, 101, 104–105,
    109, 111, 113–14, 119, 123,
    128, 147

Trepassey Bay, 55, 56, 59, 61–3

Vimy Ridge, 39

Washington DC, 84
Weybridge, 37, 39, 40, 41,
    132, 139
Wisley, 149

Ypres, 15